CARING FOR YOUR WIFE
IN SICKNESS
AND IN HEALTH

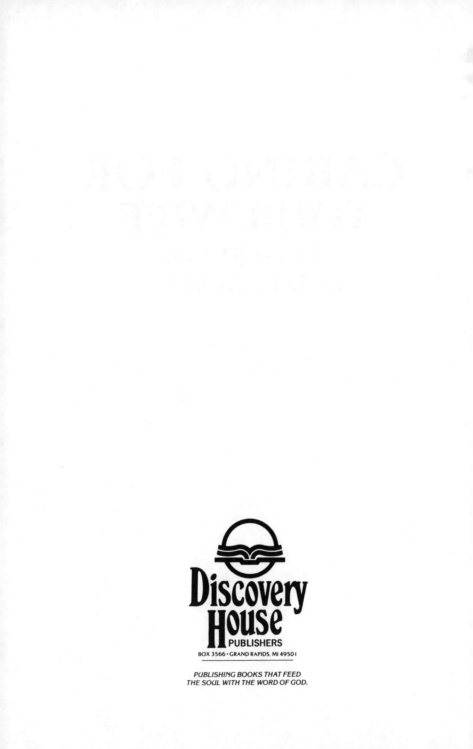

Discovery House
PUBLISHERS

BOX 3566 · GRAND RAPIDS, MI 49501

*PUBLISHING BOOKS THAT FEED
THE SOUL WITH THE WORD OF GOD.*

CARING FOR YOUR WIFE
IN SICKNESS
AND IN HEALTH

*A Husband's Guide to Understanding
the Special Health Needs of a Woman*

Richard H. Dominguez, M.D.

Library of Congress Cataloging-in-Publication Data

Dominguez, Richard H.
    Caring for your wife in sickness and in health : a husband's guide to under-
standing the special health needs of a woman / Richard H. Dominguez.
        p. cm.
    ISBN 0-929239-68-7
    1. Women—Health and hygiene. 2. Communication in marriage.
I. Title.
RA778.D66 1995
613'.04244—dc20   94-43736
                                                         CIP

Discovery House Publishers is affiliated with Radio Bible Class,
Grand Rapids, Michigan.
Discovery House books are distributed to the trade by
Thomas Nelson Publishers, Nashville, Tennessee 37214.
Printed in the United States of America
95 96 97 98 99 / CHG / 10 9 8 7 6 5 4 3 2 1

♦

*To Steve and Sanna Baker
and Carol Lou Erickson Dominguez.*

*Fear not, for I have redeemed you; I have summoned you by name;
you are mine. When you pass through the waters, I will be with you;
and when you pass through the rivers, they will not sweep over you.
When you walk through the fire, you will not be burned;
the flames will not set you ablaze (Isaiah 43:1–2).*

CONTENTS

ACKNOWLEDGMENTS

I want to thank Carol Holquist of Discovery House for her commitment to this manuscript and for giving me the opportunity to work with my Houghton College classmate Judy Markham (class of '63). I really feel fortunate that Judy agreed to edit this book, so I owe heartfelt thanks to her, to Carol, and to my daughter Jennifer Dominguez Ochs who typed the entire manuscript.

INTRODUCTION

I know it is likely that your wife bought you this book! But it wasn't written for her; this was written for you. It doesn't say "for men only," but if a woman reads it, it will be a bit like eavesdropping in the men's locker room.

This book is written for husbands who want to care for their wives. It is not politically correct, nor has any attempt been made to make it politically correct. I wrote it for men. I wrote it for you to help you understand and care for this woman you love.

I have been married to the same woman for thirty years, and we are the parents of nine children. I have seen the deaths of a younger brother, my father, my wife's parents and brother, two beloved cousins, and a nephew. I have served on the boards of two churches. So I think I can speak with some experience about the ups and downs of marriage and of life.

Even though my wife has not worked outside the home since the birth of our first child, she was our sole support for a period of time when we were first married. Also, I work closely with women in the office and at the hospital who have families to care for, and I do understand the stresses that they face. As a physician who will listen and who does care for his coworkers, I like to think that I have learned from these conversations. My spiritual mentor was a woman, my grandmother McCorkel. Four of my closest and dearest family relationships have been with women.

All of this experience has taught me to at least listen to women and hopefully to have some insight into how they think and act. This is important to understand, because we are different, guys!

After a number of years both leading and attending discussion groups at men's church retreats, I also understand how relieved and helped men are when they realize that the struggles they are having in their marriages are not unique, that the problems their wives are having are not unique, that for most of us, at times, marriage is going to be a struggle, and that none of us ever expected our wives to have health problems, yet most of us have to face this at some point or another.

I wrote this book to let you know you are not alone. In my talks with men of literally every profession and every socioeconomic category, I have learned that the problems we face are the same.

My hope and prayer for you is that you will find some useful information and tips here that will help you better care for and more fully understand this woman you love.

CHAPTER

1

In Sickness and in Health

In one of Bill Cosby's monologues he talks about marriage vows and what men and women remember about those vows. When you ask a man what he remembers, says the comedian, he will say, "Honor, love, cherish." But when you ask a woman the same question, she'll say, "Obey!"

"That's right," says Cosby. "Obey, obey, obey, obey!"

While this makes a good joke for a stand-up comic, it is no joke in real life, because this is pretty close to what most of us remember about our marriage vows. Cosby conveniently forgets about "in sickness and in health," and so do we. We remember "Love, honor, obey, and cherish," but we forget all about "in sickness and in health."

Chapter 1

How many of us even heard, let alone thought about, those words when we pledged them? We got the loving and cherishing part, but did we even consider the possibility of sickness or the importance of health? Yet for most if not all of us, at some point, sickness is going to be an issue.

Even as I write this, I remember Tom and Mary, a young couple I met during my first year in medical practice. They had only been married a couple of years when Mary developed crippling rheumatoid arthritis. She consulted with me because of a multitude of orthopedic problems resulting from complications from her arthritis. Her doctor had her on high doses of cortisone to control the inflamed joints that were disabling her, and she was already experiencing some of the side effects of long-term cortisone use.

What impressed me most during my time with this young couple was the care and devotion Tom showed his wife. She had a swollen "moon face" and was starting to develop facial hair, two of the unattractive complications of her steroid treatment, yet he treated her like a princess. Clearly his love and affection and respect for her had nothing to do with her physical appearance.

I also think of Sam and Louise, a couple who had spent all of their married life on the mission field. After thirty-nine years abroad, however, Louise developed some neurological problems, and in their fortieth year the mission board brought them home so she could have evaluation and treatment.

Louise was diagnosed with Alzheimer's disease, and she and Sam had to retire from missionary service. Within three years, Louise required full-time care from Sam. Intellectually and physically she had become a hollow shell.

With diseases such as Alzheimer's, the caregiver is frequently under more stress than the person suffering from the disease, and the churches who had supported this couple began praying for the "burdens" Sam must bear.

I'll never forget Sam's sincere response: It was not a burden to care for his dear wife, he said; it was an honor. He thanked the Lord for the opportunity to care for her.

Most of us probably read these examples with admiration, never thinking we might someday be in a similar situation ourselves. The odds are, however, that sooner or later we will be.

Our natural blindness in this regard was brought home to me a few years ago when I was asked to present a couple sessions at a men's retreat sponsored by a local church. Because of my experience with sports medicine and because it was a men's group, the young man organizing the event assumed I would want to talk about exercise or some such topic. Instead, I suggested that the men might be interested in a discussion of an issue that bore even more directly and drastically on their personal lives: how to deal with a sick wife, or how to cope when your wife is ill.

The young man, a newlywed himself, said he didn't think there would be much interest in such a topic, but we agreed to think about it further and talk again in a few days.

A week later, having done a bit of research, I told the young man that I still believed there would be a fair amount of interest in the topic and that it was the issue I wanted to present. So, with some misgivings, he scheduled me to speak on "Dealing with a Sick Wife."

We were both surprised! I had a standing-room-only crowd at both sessions! And throughout the rest of the weekend, many of the men engaged me, one on one, in meaningful dialogue on the subject.

I shouldn't have been surprised, of course. As both a doctor and a husband, I know that wives do get sick and that many men are struggling with the effects of such illnesses on them socially, emotionally, and financially. It is a common problem that men just don't talk about. Also, many of us are separated from our extended family and do not have a readily available familial support system. And I know how difficult it is, as a man, to simply arrange car pools, much less get your children fed, dressed, off to school—and then go to work and effectively do your own job. I also know that in most families where the wife works, her illness can have a significant financial impact.

I know from personal experience—and this was rein-forced at the men's retreat—that most men don't feel they have anyone they can talk to about these problems. Most men don't have an emotional support system of intimate friends. If you ask a man who his best friend is, he will probably say, "My wife."

Now I can hear some of you saying, "But what about the fact that women live longer than men as a rule?" Yes, the irony is that your wife will probably outlive you. But statis-tics show that during your life together, she will be sick more often and see the doctor more than you will.

For example, depression is three times as common in women as in men; at least 12 percent of all American women are stricken with breast cancer; and a staggering 75 percent suffer some disabling symptoms during menopause. Visit almost any doctor's waiting room and you will find that the majority of patients are women.

Women also frequently need to seek a physician's help for things that technically might not be considered an illness. Many young women need medical care because of difficulties and symptoms associated with their monthly hormonal cycle and menstruation or the abnormalities of their cycle. And then, of course, there is pregnancy. While it is a "state of health," not an illness, there are illnesses and complications related to pregnancy that can be quite debilitating; even a "normal pregnancy" can at times cause disabling symptoms. Later in life, the other great hormonal change that occurs in women, menopause, can have profound emotional and physical symptoms that need to be treated by a doctor. In fact, there is a whole special area of medicine designed to care for these "women only" problems.

In other words, most of us men, at some time or other, will have to deal with our wives' illnesses and the impact of those illnesses on our marriages and home life.

THE THREE STRESSORS

Experts and counselors maintain that there are three major stressors in marriage and that almost all marriage problems result from one or more of these three: money, time, and sex. If your wife becomes ill, you will immediately have to face all three of these stressors.

Money

One of the first things newly married couples have to learn to deal with is family finances. It is unusual for both husband and wife to have the same approach to money. Differences in background, frugality, spending habits, and how we value money usually lead to the first "fights" or first major difficulties that need to be worked out in a marriage. Most married couples go through this process. But financial difficulties can crop up at any time and can continue to be a major stressor in a marriage.

Time

When we were dating, we could hardly find enough time to be together while living separately. That's one of the reasons we got married! But once we're married, it's surprising how little time we actually have to spend together.

Early on, the demands of continuing education, different work schedules, and fatigue all conspire to keep us apart. When we were dating, we had to work at being together, and we knew and accepted that; but when we got married we expected to have all the time in the world with each other—and suddenly we find that is not the case. We still have to work at it.

Time constraints can be a major stressor in a marriage. Pressured by fear that they won't advance in their profession or won't be successful on the job, men and women spend more and more time at work. Then come the children. While time spent nurturing them is "precious time," it nonetheless can keep husband and wife from having much time together. And this doesn't even begin to take into account all the other demands on time in our pressure cooker society.

Sex

The third stressor in a marriage is sex. Let's face it, guys: one of the reasons we wanted to get married in the first place was an overwhelming desire and passion to be physically intimate with the woman we love. There is no question that sexual desires are very strong in young men. This is true for young women also, but usually to a different degree and intensity than we expected. The best analogy I've heard is that sexual desire and performance in men is like cooking with a microwave, whereas in women it is like cooking with a crockpot!

Sex can't—and shouldn't—be rushed. But if you are under time constraints or if you have been arguing about money or struggling over financial issues, this can have an impact on your sex life.

Many other factors can affect your sex life, and since this is an integral part of your life together as well as your individual identities, when either one or both of you are frustrated with the sexual side of marriage, that becomes a stressor.

THE STRESSOR OF ILLNESS

If the husband is sick, it is natural for the wife to nurture and care for him. Many women find caring for a sick husband to be a way of expressing emotional and some physical intimacy and don't, at least in the short term, feel sexually deprived.

While most men are more than happy to care for a sick wife and will do it out of love and compassion, few find it gratifying or fulfilling, especially in a physical or sexual sense.

As a rule, women are able to handle a husband's illness much better than men are able to handle a wife's illness.

More than likely, the wife is the one who arranges the car pools and the day care and the baby-sitting and the day-to-day household affairs. Even when she works outside the home, these matters are arranged around her schedule, not her husband's. Many of us have freely dumped these responsibilities on our wives. So if they are sick, we may find it difficult and stressful to have to take over these family duties.

A wife's illness can also cause financial stress. First there is the cost of the illness itself. Then in many homes, both husband and wife work, frequently out of financial necessity, so her illness can affect family income. If she works part-time, she may not have disability insurance or paid sick leave. When she doesn't work, she isn't paid.

The family is under assault today from many directions, and most ministers are not reticent to voice this fact from the pulpit. Yet I have never heard a minister talk about the stresses that a spouse's illness places on a marriage and a family. Countless Christian books have been written to extol marriage and how to make it better, but none of them seem to deal with the reality of illness and its impact on a relationship.

MEN AS CAREGIVERS

In our culture men are portrayed as uncaring takers or leavers. In other words, men take what they can from marriage, and if the marriage is not what they want it to be, they leave. In fact, caring is seen almost solely as a feminine trait.

Just think about our movie heroes, past or present: John Wayne, James Bond, Sylvester Stallone, Bruce Willis, or Steven Seagal. What do they have in common? They are all heroic warriors. If they are injured or wounded, they sew themselves up or suffer silently and keep on going, always against incredible odds. And if they are cared for by someone, that someone is always female. If I asked you to name actors who have played the roles of caring, nurturing males, I'm willing to bet that only one name would come to mind: Alan Alda.

More often, we see depictions such as the recent made-for-TV movie that told the story of a man whose wife developed multiple sclerosis, a crippling neurological disease. The woman became so disabled that her husband had to hire a full-time nurse to care for her. And, of course, you guessed it: the husband eventually ran off with the nurse.

If the wife is sick, injured, or disabled, chances are the husband is portrayed as insensitive, selfish, or a deserter rather than a loving, sensitive, caring hero.

Some of this media-driven perception may be fallout from the radical feminist movement, which has tended to portray all men as oppressors and abusers. The power of ideas sometimes makes it difficult to separate perception from reality.

Contrary to this, many men—many men I know personally—are caring, compassionate, giving people. Most of my friends are loving husbands and fathers. But the fact of the matter is, women are often more loving and caring than men.

This is a complex subject, and I don't pretend to have all the answers. However, I do believe God has gifted women with the ability to care and nurture. What they learn from their mothers in this regard helps reinforce and enhance this God-given talent. And while men certainly have the ability to be caregivers, I'm not sure whether they have it to a lesser degree than women or whether it just doesn't bubble to the surface as naturally.

I must confess, I'm always shocked when I hear of a woman leaving her family, and I am always impressed by men who have been left with their children and have faithfully raised them alone. I see many of these single fathers in my office, and I am impressed by the compassion, care, and love they show their children.

Are little girls taught more about caring and nurturing than little boys? Do mothers spend more time teaching their daughters how to care and nurture than they do their sons? Do sons copy their fathers' approach to caring and compassion?

I guess those are questions for social scientists to debate. My main concern here is how we men can be better caregivers right now and from here on out. Because, you see, I speak not just as a physician, but as a Christian husband who has walked through the shadows where some of you are right now. And I want to share some of the lessons I have learned along the way, in hopes that they will benefit you.

Chapter 1

I don't have all the answers, but I think I do have some, and I want to help you better understand your wife and communicate with her, and thus strengthen both your ability as a caregiver and your marriage. I also want you to begin sharing honestly with your Christian brothers about these matters. This will not only help them spiritually, but will help you and help your marriage.

One of the things I have come to realize is that most men don't expect their wives to be sick. And since it is a topic that is rarely if ever talked about, we tend to think we are the only ones who are facing the problem of having a sick wife. Not only that, but most of us have not developed the emotional and social support mechanisms that most women have. This leads to a sense of isolation and frustration, which only adds to the stress that is already present when you have a sick wife.

My hope and prayer is that this book will help you become a better caregiver, help you learn how to take care of yourself, and help you realize that you are not alone.

CHAPTER

2

We Never Expected This!

My wife, Judy, and I met when we were both students at Houghton College, working in the dining hall as waiter and waitress. I was dating Judy's roommate, and Judy was dating someone, so we just became good friends, often eating together at the end of our dining hall shift. Near the end of my last year at Houghton, we laughingly agreed that if ten years from then we weren't married to anyone else, we should probably marry each other.

The next year I started medical school at the University of Chicago, and at the end of that year my relationship with Judy's roommate ended. A year later, near the end of my second year in med school, Judy wrote and invited me to visit her in New Jersey, where she was teaching.

Chapter 2

For a Christian, the University of Chicago was a lonely place, so later that year I happily hopped into my trusty VW and drove out to Jersey to visit Judy Wickware—and from then on our friendship developed into a deep love for each other.

Between my junior and senior years in medical school we got married, and we had a great time that first year. Our second year of marriage, however, was very difficult for Judy. That was my first year of internship at the University of Washington in Seattle, and I was gone every other night on duty. Seattle can be a dreary place in the winter if you don't have time to go to the mountains and ski—and we didn't. Judy was teaching on Mercer Island, which meant that she drove to work in the dark and the rain and came home in the dark and the rain, often to an empty house. She now remarks that she cried herself to sleep every other night.

In 1967 we returned to the University of Chicago where I did a year of orthopedic residency, and in July of 1968 our first child, Jennifer, was born. Then in August of that year I entered the Air Force.

Like most of the physicians of my generation, I found my medical training interrupted by the Vietnam War. But I was fortunate; my "war experience" was comfortable and safe. I served two years at March Air Force Base and received residency training credit for it. Our second daughter, Heather, was born there.

March Air Force Base is located outside Riverside, California, halfway between L.A. and Palm Springs near the mountains. Our two years there were two of the best years of our married life. My hours in the Air Force were very regular and predictable, and Judy and I discovered that we are warm weather people. We traveled all over southern California with the girls and had plenty of time together.

20

We returned to Chicago in August 1970. I'll never forget that day. The thermometers on the south side of Chicago registered 100 degrees in what felt like 100 percent humidity. Judy, who was pregnant with our third child, found the heat and humidity oppressive; this, in contrast to the idyllic southern California climate we had come to love, and combined with the high-rise city around us, gave her a very closed-in feeling.

Sam, our third child, was born in October, three months after our return from California. After his birth, Judy was a bit "blue," and I was not prepared for this. With our first two children she had been so upbeat, handling pregnancy well. After Jennifer's birth Judy had been a bit depressed but that was to be expected. Jennifer had been premature and was hospitalized in the preemie nursery for several weeks. That period of depression seemed mild, short, and inconsequential. After Heather's birth, everything had been fine.

Yet Judy's reaction was fairly easy to understand. We now had three little kids, we were living in an apartment that was smaller than we were accustomed to, and we were no longer in sunny California. Along with this, I was back working ridiculous residency hours rather than the regulated Air Force routine. I was gone early in the morning and didn't return home until late in the evening, and every other night I usually didn't come home at all because I was on call. I worked every Saturday until at least noon and almost every Sunday.

As time passed, however, Judy's depression didn't let up, and along with it she developed a multitude of physical ailments. Because of the multiplicity of symptoms, we sought help from several specialists at the University of Chicago. Unable to find a physical source, they recommended that she see a psychiatrist.

The psychiatrist Judy consulted diagnosed her problem as severe depression and strongly recommended hospitalization. As if that news weren't enough of a shock, the morning after her appointment with the psychiatrist, Judy witnessed a mugging while she and the girls were coming home from the supermarket. An elderly woman was mugged in front of our house and almost in front of Judy. Although there had been no threat to her or the children, Judy was traumatized and shaken. The fact that it happened in front of her and right in front of our apartment was shocking and terrifying to her. This compounded her problems. She was afraid to go outside, feeling like a prisoner in our apartment, further deepening her depression.

The idea of hospitalizing Judy in a psychiatric ward was stressful for both of us, to say the least, so we explored other alternatives. Fortunately, through some friends at the Christian Medical Society, we learned about a Christian psychiatrist and his wife, a psychiatric social worker, who functioned as a team. After evaluating Judy, they said they were willing to treat her on an outpatient basis.

Judy responded well after a couple weeks of treatment, and the psychiatrist started her on what was then a new drug, Sinequan. She was on this periodically for many months, but was finally able to come off it permanently.

About the same time, with the aid of the G.I. bill and a five-hundred-dollar down payment, we bought a small four-bedroom bungalow in the suburban community of Glen Ellyn. With the help of the husband-wife psychiatric team, the medication, and our moving out of the city, Judy's depression slowly lifted and our lives got back on a more even keel.

During those months of this first depression, however, there were times when I despaired of ever having a normal relationship with Judy or a normal marriage. I really had no idea how to deal with her illness and be a supportive and loving husband in the midst of it. It wasn't that I didn't love her; I just didn't know how. But I never thought of asking for help. Basically, I just tried to work around "the problem," even though we had three kids in diapers. I didn't ask for any help at work, where I was putting in full shifts at the hospital and then moonlighting to help pay the medical bills. Once or twice a week, when my residency duties were done, I would go on to an emergency room at another hospital and work the night shift. In the morning I'd go straight back to my residency duties without ever getting home.

Working harder and longer hours to earn more money seemed normal to me. That was something my father had done; in fact, that's what my mother had done every Christmas. She normally did not work outside the home, but every year during the holiday season she took a part-time job to help pay for Christmas. To me, moonlighting for extra money was just a natural, proper way to take care of my family and pay the bills. The thought of borrowing money never occurred to me. I had worked all through college and medical school and finished both with no debts. I was so used to working long, extra hours and one or two extra jobs that borrowing money so that I could spend more time at home never occurred to me.

After I finished my residency, I joined a group practice in Glen Ellyn. This didn't move us up the economic ladder right away, since my combined residency pay and moonlighting pay nearly equaled my initial income in medical practice, but at least our lifestyle was a bit more sane. Several years later I accepted an invitation to form a new practice that became a growing, successful, gratifying venture professionally. I was very happy with my practice, Judy and I seemed to be sailing along fine in our marriage, and our children were active and healthy and starting school. After Matthew, our fourth child, was born, we had even moved into our "dream house" with an indoor pool. We were involved in a good church and had established a circle of friends, some of them old friends from our college days. We were living the American dream.

Judy became pregnant with our fifth child, and the pregnancy was going well. Then one day, when she was about six months along, she called me at the office.

"Richard, I'm scared. I keep falling over trying to crawl to the bathroom," she said.

"When did this start, Judy?" I said. "I didn't even know you were sick!"

"I didn't want to worry you. I just haven't been feeling good for a few days, but today things have really gotten worse."

I told her I would be home immediately.

I knew something must be wrong neurologically for this to be happening, and within a short time I had her in the emergency room, where they hospitalized her immediately.

The diagnosis came clear a day or so later. She had viral encephalitis, an inflammation and infection involving the brain. There are no known treatments for this infection; one simply "supports" the patient. This meant watching Judy, making sure she continued to breathe, and hoping and praying for the best. Over the next two weeks I watched her deteriorate daily.

Now I had a wife in the hospital, desperately ill, and four little children at home. But this time the difference was as dramatic as the situation.

My partners in the practice pitched in, cutting me all the slack I needed so I could work at a reduced level that allowed me to get home and be with the children regularly and visit

Judy frequently. But equally if not more important was the fact that my extended family was around now. My parents had moved back to the Chicago area from upstate New York and were living in a nearby suburb, so my mother and father moved into our home to help me with the children and to be there for emotional support. Both my sisters were also nearby now, and one of my brothers was now in law practice in Wheaton. What an enormous difference it made to have a large extended family around.

At no time do we need the support of family and friends more than at times of illness. Yet the irony is that many people don't want to—or can't—deal with the hard reality of a deteriorating, ongoing illness.

On a regular basis friends and acquaintances would ask me, "How's your wife doing?" or "How *is* Judy?"

I would respond honestly. "She's worse. She's deteriorating daily." Then I would thank them sincerely for their obvious concern.

My honesty became so uncomfortable for them, though, it was as if I were kicking them in the stomach or punching them in the nose. I could almost see them flinch. It was clear that they wanted me to say, "Better, thank you," or, "Okay, thanks for asking." Even the physicians and nurses I worked with, people who dealt with the reality of illness day in and day out, had difficulty dealing with a colleague who was facing bad news.

Part of the problem is our American mind-set. Failure is a nasty word; we always think that things are going to get better or that we are going to win or overcome or achieve. Even much of the preaching we hear teaches us how to be winners, how to be "successful prayer warriors," with the implication being that we will always get "positive answers." The fact is, the reality is, that people do get sick, and sometimes they don't get better. Sometimes they get worse. Sometimes they die.

Ironically, part of the burden of illness is dealing with other people's discomfort with your bad news or a deteriorating situation.

For two weeks Judy got worse. Although the baby she carried seemed to be doing fine, Judy was in agony. Encephalitis is swelling of the brain and it is very painful as it stretches the sensitive tissue covering the brain. She pleaded for relief from the excruciating headaches, but we were unable to give her any medication to alleviate the pain. Any medicine for pain relief would endanger her life. With the increased pressure on the brain, any type of sedation could cause her to lapse into unconsciousness or stop breathing. Also, we did not know what the effect might be on the unborn child.

At her lowest ebb, for three days in a row Judy pleaded with me to put her out of her pain-filled misery, to overdose her with medication. Judy is a strong Christian; she is adamantly opposed to euthanasia and is strongly pro-life. But even Christians who would normally never contemplate such a thing may cry out or plead, "I want to be dead!" when in excruciating pain. It's a reflection of the severity of the pain, not a change in their moral stance. While she seemed coherent, Judy really was delirious with pain. (I would add that Judy does not remember this and denies ever having said such a thing. While her body was crying out in pain, she was in a coma and doesn't remember any of it.)

Much prayer was being offered, however, and God answered mercifully. Judy's pain started to lessen and she began to recover. Within ten days she was able to leave the hospital and be cared for at home. She had been in the hospital a month.

Near the end of her hospitalization, Judy began to have contractions and go into premature labor. They were able to suppress the labor, but it began again after she got home. Within a week she was back in the hospital, this time to deliver our son Nathan. Because of the residuals of the encephalitis she was unable to hold him or feed him, and at first he had difficulty sucking, so they were both in the hospital for about a week. When they came home, my youngest sister, Kay, moved in with us and helped care for Judy and Nathan.

Six months later I came home from work and Judy announced, "I'm better. This is the first time since I got sick that I feel good." The encephalitis was finally gone and she felt good. Six months later!

Today, Judy and I still have a friendly argument about those days. She denies ever saying that she wanted to be put out of her misery. She also does not remember those three days at all. I do. And whenever I see Dr. Kevorkian on TV or hear a discussion about assisted suicide, my mind flashes back to my beloved wife lying there in agony, pleading for me to help her end her own life. What if I had? . . .

When Judy and I promised to love and honor each other, in sickness and in health, we never anticipated anything like this. We were young and in love. We were also naive. We didn't have any comprehension that not only were we bringing two unique individuals into that wonderful equation that becomes a marriage; we were also bringing our parents, our siblings, our grandparents—everything that makes us who we are.

None of us stand as separate entities. All of us are a sum of our environment, our upbringing, and our heredity, and we bring all of these, along with our unique individual selves, into our marriages.

Chapter 2

I grew up in a Christian home, the oldest of seven children. My father's sister married my mother's brother, so I also have six double first cousins who are almost as close to me as brothers and sisters. I was born and raised in Chicago, where my family lived close to Jewish neighborhoods. I always felt we had a great deal in common with our Jewish neighbors since, my family being devout Seventh Day Baptists, we worshiped on the same day, Saturday. When I was in my teens, my parents switched to the Wesleyan Methodist Church, and suddenly Sunday was our Sabbath!

My paternal grandfather emigrated from Spain to Mexico, where he met and married my grandmother, of Indian descent. At age eighteen my father moved to Chicago, where he met and married my mother, a Macorkel of Pennsylvania Dutch extraction.

My father was the classic Hispanic male—tall, good-looking, hardworking, and stoical. From him I learned that men do not cry. Men do not complain. Men do not talk about how they feel, and men never admit to pain. Men are providers. Men never publicly show affection, especially to their male children. That was the heritage I grew up with—the classic macho male.

I loved and respected my father, but I can't remember having any heart-to-heart talks with him or his giving me much fatherly advice. He always worked evenings or nights, so I rarely saw him during the week. He did everything he could to provide for us, but he tended to spoil the girls and strongly discipline us boys. He refused to show affection to his sons and refused to let my mother publicly show affection to us, at least in his presence.

Judy grew up in a very different kind of home. She had only one brother, and her father was an alcoholic. While he eventually quit and joined AA, he died at a relatively early age, sixty-seven, from complications of years of drinking and heavy smoking. Judy's brother also died at a very early age, forty-seven, from complications of alcoholism.

Judy now remembers first being depressed in college when her parents told her they were divorcing, which they never did. The fact that her father and brother were alcoholics was never spoken of, so there were many "secrets" in her family. She felt isolated and hated being at home.

After the death of her mother in 1988, Judy began to realize and face the effects of being raised in a family with an alcoholic father, with the aid of a self-help group called ACOA (Adult Children of Alcoholics). While this helped her understand some of the reasons behind the way she feels and behaves at times and her recurring bouts of depression, she continues to deal with frustration and loss and the fact that she was never really able to communicate with her mother, father, and brother.

Judy and I have been through many tough things in our twenty-nine years of marriage. We have had our joys and our sorrows, our ups and downs, our bad times and our good times. Through it all, though, we have both grown, and today we have a stronger, better marriage because of it.

But we are not unique. Many of you have gone through or are going through trials in your own marriages; and if you have not yet, you will to one degree or another. Trust me on that. Every couple goes through times of stress and difficulty and illness. Marriage (and life) is not a sitcom on TV where in twenty-four minutes everything is solved every week.

The important thing is that you face these stressful times together, honestly, and learn to cope in a healthy way. Believe me, your marriage will be stronger and you will love and care for your wife in ways you would never even have dreamed possible that day you walked down the aisle together.

CHAPTER

3

Vive la Différence

"The only difference between men and women is that men never listen to what women say and women never forget anything that men say" (Ellen, a nurse).

"It's not fair, Dad. You men don't have to put up with this every month" (One of my daughters as a teenager, lying on a couch doubled over with menstrual cramps).

"Men don't know what pain is because they have never given birth to a child" (A female proverb).

"You just don't understand" (Deborah Tannen, author).

"What this country needs is more men who act and lead like Margaret Thatcher," said one British citizen, speaking about the U.K. This could also be said of the U.S. Whether you agreed with her policies and politics or not, Margaret Thatcher was a great leader—and a woman.

As men and women, created in His image, we are all equal in God's eyes—and, for that matter, in the eyes of the United States Constitution. But when it comes to intelligence and leadership ability, there are many women who surpass most men. In my medical school class at the University of Chicago, for example, there were seventy-two of us. Of that seventy-two, five were women, all of whom were superior intellectually, artistically, musically, and athletically. So I am very familiar with superior women. Some of my earliest childhood memories are of times spent with my sisters and several female cousins, who were all better than I was in art, athletics, and certain academic areas. My cousin Linda has a Ph.D. from the University of Michigan and is a national authority on reading. My sister Marge owns a successful real estate agency. I have never considered girls or women the "weaker sex." Women are not inferior. That is fact!

Yet men and women are different. This has nothing to do with superiority or inferiority. It has to do with differences. And there are at least three significant differences between men and women.

THREE DIFFERENCES

The first and most obvious is *physical* . Men and women don't look the same. Even at an early age boys and girls learn to tell the difference. And the physical difference isn't only visual. The best women athletes in any sport are usually at least 10 percent weaker, slower, or less effective than the best male athletes.

Having said this, I would also state that there are very few people reading this book, male or female, who could beat Chris Evert or Steffi Graf at tennis. And there are very few men who could beat Nancy Lopez at golf or swim faster than Janet Evans or run faster than Florence Griffith-Joyner. But on an even playing field, best against best, the physical differences matter. When you compare time standards in any sport where there is a time standard, such as track and field or swimming, there is usually a 10 percent difference between males and females.

The second area of difference is *hormonal* . Any physician or student of physiology can tell you that the hormones in males and females are different. Interestingly enough, the major sex hormones, testosterone in the male and estrogen in the female, are present in all of us in different degrees. Normally, females have a small amount of testosterone and males have a small amount of estrogen. But there are other hormones, especially progesterone, that females have and males don't.

Hormones can affect the way we feel, and while they tend to be fairly steady in the male, hormones do fluctuate in the female. This is particularly true once women begin menstruating, and until they stop completely some women experience a monthly fluctuation that can radically affect their feelings and their moods. That is fact!

The male sex hormone, testosterone, in high doses can cause hostility and violent aggressive behavior, triggered by the slightest cause. This is one of the reasons athletes who take anabolic steroids do some crazy things. Men who take these steroids "feel good" and like the way they look. Because of this, they are tempted to increase the dosage so that they feel better and look better and get bigger. This increased level of steroids leads to wild mood swings and increasingly aggressive or out-of-control behavior. Since some muscle atrophy occurs fairly quickly upon cessation, men who stop anabolic steroids frequently panic as they see themselves "shrinking." Withdrawal from steroids has even led some young men to suicide.

The female hormones, estrogen and progesterone, also affect a person's mood or sense of well-being. Between the ages of forty-seven and fifty-five, most women begin the transitional period called menopause. For 25 percent, one out of four, there is no appreciable change in how they feel, behave, or act. Their period stops and life goes on. But in the other 75 percent, three out of four, unpleasant or difficult symptoms occur that are clearly related to the hormonal changes going on in these women. These affect a woman's mood and the way she relates to those around her.

Hormones affect women in other ways also. Breast cancer in many cases is hormone related, and 12 percent of all women face breast cancer at some point in their lives. Hormones can also play a role in depression, which may account for the fact that depression is three times as common in women as in men. There is an entire branch of medicine that specializes in medical and physical problems of women. There is no such thing for men.

The third difference between men and women is *the way they communicate,* and it begins early.

Teachers and educators have known for years that young girls are more "verbal" than boys. Not only do they use words better, but they also feel a stronger need to communicate and establish relationships. Whether men and women communicate differently and if that is a genetic or sexually inherited difference or a learned experience is an ongoing debate. Is it really a difference in the way we communicate or is it more than that? Is it an emotional difference that exists, and words are just one way we communicate that emotional difference?

Women start using words to communicate emotions early on and continue to do so throughout their lives. From the time they are little girls, women talk to each other; they share feelings and dreams; they use language as a means not only of communication, but of sharing emotional experiences. Talking is a way of drawing together, of being friends, of understanding each other.

Men, on the other hand, use language as a means of battling, of sparring. Little boys say things like, "My dad is bigger than your dad," or, "My dad can beat up your dad."

For men, language is a way to gain position or status; it is used to keep someone apart from you. Just listen to the all-talk sports radio stations, a venue that is predominantly male, where men brag about their team, their coach, their player, and where they put down the other team, the other coach, the other player.

"Trash talk" started as a way to establish athletic dominance, using language to gain an advantage and goad an opponent on the field or on the court: "I can score on you at will." . . . "I'll stuff your shot down your throat if you come this way." Trash talk uses language to irritate and brag and talk *at*, not with, an opponent, and it's a male thing.

Money talk is another way men establish dominance. How much a man makes is a way of keeping score and, unfortunately, is one of the main ways that many men judge each other. Another is athletic prowess. The more athletic you are or the more money you make, the more self-worth you have as a male.

When you think of a "power lunch," you don't think of sitting down in a homey cafe over a cup of coffee and a piece of pie, chatting away and getting to know each other. A power lunch connotes men in expensive suits with red silk ties trying to cut megadeals or stomp down the opposition.

Most women don't hesitate to share their intimate feelings, whether they have been hurt, wounded, or humiliated.

They talk openly and freely about relationships. They have no problem sharing their concerns about their spouse's behavior, his follies, or his unhappiness over his job.

When men get together we want to brag about our wives or our conquests. We don't want to talk about our feelings—and we especially don't want to admit that we have been hurt by something in our relationship. Most of us wouldn't dream of sitting around saying, "Man, my wife has PMS again and it wrecked our weekend." And we would never, ever talk about how we "feel" about our wife having PMS.

While men may extol the virtues of the "strong, silent type," most women hate the "silent type"—the man who can't communicate. The worst thing a girl can say to another girl about a guy is that "he doesn't talk."

But the fact that women communicate and men don't is just part of the problem. Because even when men do talk, their words mean different things. In fact, I sometimes think it's a wonder we communicate at all!

Let me give you two examples from my own experience. I think they'll sound familiar.

First scenario: What do you do when your wife comes home with a new haircut?

Who knows?

You're dead if you don't notice the haircut immediately, but worse yet, if you do notice it, there is almost nothing you can say that is going to be right. You can say you like it, you can try and think of some creative thing like "It's cute, it's you" (although I have trouble believing any man would say "It's you"). Or you can opt for the vague, always-subject-to-misunderstanding "It's different." But trust me—you can't win this one. Whatever you say doesn't matter, because the reaction you give nonverbally, whether it is surprise, shock, pleasure, or indifference is going to be the important thing.

In other words, regarding haircuts, there is nothing you can say that is correct, but you have got to say something.

Second scenario: What do you do when your wife says, "Don't get me anything for my birthday (anniversary, Christmas, whatever) because things are tight right now and I know we don't have a lot of money and I don't want you to waste any money on me"?

The worst thing any man can do is take those words at face value. What those words really mean is "Money is tight, I appreciate that, and you don't have to get me anything expensive, but don't you dare forget my birthday."

Women tend to be interdependent, and for them "trouble talk" is a ritual. "I understand, I know what you have been through." Language creates intimacy, and talk is what holds relationships together. For a woman, a relationship is where she is free to talk.

Men want to be independent, and language keeps people from pushing them around. Men don't like to be told what to do, which is one of the reasons they don't ask for directions—even when they're lost!

So we need to dispel the myth that there are no differences between the sexes. But just because we are different doesn't mean one is better than or worth more than the other. If we are to understand each other and grow in our relationships together, however, we must understand those differences and learn to deal with them, because those differences affect all of our life together. Nowhere is this more evident than when illness strikes.

CHAPTER

4

He Said,
She Said

In one of his early movies, *Cool Hand Luke,* Paul Newman plays a juvenile delinquent who does something that most of us have probably fantasized about doing at one time or another: he walks down the street with a pipe cutter, cutting all the parking meters off their stands. Later, when he is caught, tried, convicted, and sent to jail, the old southern sheriff utters the classic line, "What we have here is a failure to communicate."

That's exactly what men and women have much of the time. Or possibly, since we must have communicated something, somehow, or we wouldn't have gotten married, perhaps it is more accurate to say that what we have is a "breakdown in communication."

Twice since we've been married my wife has made me go to the ear doctor and have my hearing checked because she was convinced I was going deaf. My hearing always checks out perfectly; I can hear fine. But "not hearing" is a common male trait.

When my daughters were little they would sometimes climb up on my lap, grab my face with both hands, and aim my face at them and talk to me. They knew that was what it took to communicate when Dad was concentrating on something else or watching sports on TV!

My friends in ear, nose, and throat practice tell me I am not an unusual case. Husbands are always being forced by their wives to come in and have their hearing checked. It is, they say, a common reason men come to have their hearing tested—and almost always their hearing tests out fine.

It's not that we *can't* hear. It's that we *don't* hear because we are not listening!

WHAT DOES IT TAKE TO COMMUNICATE?

Communication begins with listening. My wife gets totally frustrated when she tells me something and then discovers I haven't heard a word she's said. And I know I'm not the only man who does this.

Part of my problem—and perhaps you will be able to identify with this—is that all day long I listen to people and I have to pay close attention to every word they say and how they say it because the essence of medical diagnosis is history-taking and talking to patients. Most of the time my examinations simply confirm what the patient told me. So after all this intent and intense listening, I just want to tune out. Sound familiar?

But if you have small children at home and your wife is not working outside the home, then she has been listening to "mama, dada, poopoo" all day long. She is longing for some adult conversation.

Or, if she works outside the home, your wife may be just as tired of listening to other people's problems as you are. She may want *you* to listen to what has happened during her day.

Whatever the case, at the end of the day you very likely have two individuals looking forward to two different evenings. Let's take the first as an example, because it is a scene I am very familiar with.

Your wife is looking forward to having an adult conversation; you are talked out. You want to sit down, relax, and have some peace and quiet; she wants to have a real conversation. This is not a formula for great communication.

Depending on circumstances, this can be even more complicated. Especially if she greets you with, "Hi, hon. How was your day?" and the only options you have are "Terrible," "Great," or "Okay."

Physicians, for example, have to protect patient confidentiality, so I can't talk about the details of my work. The same is true for attorneys, accountants, counselors, and certain other professionals.

I have a friend who works for the CIA, and he can't talk about his work *at all*. As a matter of fact, he won't even admit he works for the CIA. Of course, it doesn't take much of a sleuth to figure out where someone works when he won't tell you where he works but you know he works in Langley, Virginia, and you know he works for the government! But at any rate, the guy just can't talk about his work. This is true for many professionals.

So when it comes to communicating, how do we get started?

Communication experts say the best way is to repeat what you heard the other person say. I've discovered that this is very effective. It takes some practice, and your spouse may get mad at you at first, but it will help you learn to listen.

It works something like this:

You've come home from work, you've changed into your sweats, and you're deciding whether you should mow the lawn or tune in to the Bulls' play-off game on ESPN when you hear your wife say, "Paul and Barb Jones are breaking up and she is very upset about it."

You repeat that back to her, and she says, "What are you talking about? That's not what I said at all! I said Paul and Barb are having their patio broken up and the landscaper broke both glass patio doors and Barb is very upset about it."

Now that may be an extreme example, but it's the kind of thing that happens a lot—at least to me!

In other words, you can't communicate if you don't listen. And you can't listen if you don't focus.

The minute you—one or both of you—walk in the door usually is not the best time to do that. So my advice is for the two of you to sit down and agree on a time when you can talk at the end of the day. You should choose a quiet time when the two of you will not be interrupted. Whatever you do, make time to talk and to listen.

Here are "ten commandments" I have found helpful in learning and practicing the art of communication.

TEN COMMANDMENTS FOR COMMUNICATING

First commandment: *Talk to your spouse at least once a day!*

Find at least fifteen minutes a day when the two of you can talk alone, uninterrupted by children or the phone. Obviously some days your schedules just will not permit this, but work toward this goal. If you don't make a commitment to do this, it won't happen.

If you are a young couple, you will soon discover that as your family increases, this becomes exponentially more difficult. It is tough to find time alone together when you have one child; it is four times as difficult when you have two. It is sixteen times as difficult with three—and so on.

By the time Judy and I had four children, months would go by when we did not have effective communication. Between my schedule and hers, carpooling, schooling, and a million other everyday things, it was very difficult to find time to talk when one of us wasn't falling asleep. I didn't even realize this was happening until the two of us were able to go away to a medical meeting and started *talking*, alone together, in our hotel room. After that, for a period in our lives, we made a point of going away to a medical meeting every three months just so we could talk.

If you can't talk at home on a regular basis, go out on "dates"; once a week or every other week go to a movie or to dinner or to the theater (even if your communication is great, the two of you should have special times alone together). Just the time alone in the car going back and forth will provide you with an opportunity to start talking to each other. If that doesn't work, get away for a weekend once a month, or even one Saturday a month. Whatever you do, don't go more than three months without spending some time alone together.

I hate the term "quality time" because I don't think it is valid. You can't turn on a switch and suddenly have quality communication or experiences. You need to spend *quantity time*; out of that, quality time will develop. This is just as true with your wife as it is with your children. It's sort of like panning for gold: you have to sift a lot of sand to find a nugget or two.

Second commandment: *Exercise together at least thirty minutes at least three times a week.*

This basic formula for physical fitness is not only good for you physically and mentally, but also can dramatically improve your communication.

You and your wife should exercise together as much as possible, whether it is walking or jogging, tennis or golf, swimming, skiing, or biking. This accomplishes two things: it gets you both the exercise you need, and it gives you time alone together to talk. And if your wife is a stay-at-home homemaker, it will get her out of the house.

When our friends William and Pat took up golfing, I asked William why. He said it was the only way the two of them could get alone and talk. Golf is an great game for that.

Having said this, I also recognize that you may not be able to agree on an exercise to do together, or one of you may not want to exercise. You cannot force another person to exercise; all you can do is create the opportunity.

Third commandment: *Baby-sit at least once a week.*

This frees your wife to do something she wants to do and gives you time alone with your children. Encourage your spouse to do something she enjoys.

Fourth commandment: *Encourage your wife to participate in your church's women's retreats, Bible studies, small groups, and other opportunities for spiritual fellowship and growth.* (Wives, if you are reading this, do the same for your husbands.)

Solve all the baby-sitting and logistic problems yourself and don't have a messy house waiting for her when she returns.

Trust me, you will communicate better if both of you have a chance to grow as individuals and to interact with members of the same sex. You will find that you are not alone in your frustrations or concerns, and you will make new friends; all of this will certainly improve your ability to communicate.

Fifth commandment: *Share in meal preparation.*

This is especially true if your wife works outside the home. If it is difficult for you to be home in time to help with preparing the meal, then at least do the cleanup and share the grocery shopping detail. And if you do cook, clean up your mess; don't leave the kitchen in such a state of disaster that it is more work for her to clean up your mess than to have prepared the meal in the first place.

Ignorance is no excuse. Today's supermarkets offer a multitude of frozen entrées and deli selections, and anybody can fix a fresh salad. And there is always McDonald's, Burger King, or Little Caesar's Pizza!

Sixth commandment: *Pick up your clothes—yea, even all your children for generations shall pick up their clothes.*

Nothing is more demeaning than treating your wife like a locker room attendant. She shouldn't let you get away with it anyhow, and you shouldn't let your children get away with it at all!

Trust me on this: you can communicate better with someone you treat with respect and someone who realizes you respect her.

Seventh commandment: *Help with the laundry—and your children, junior high and up, shall do their own laundry for generations to come.*

Don't permit your children to rag their mother about undone laundry when they should be doing it themselves. It doesn't take a rocket scientist to sort whites and colors and learn what to bleach and what not to. What is true of commandment six is also true of commandment seven. Respect aids communication.

Eighth commandment: *Thou shalt vacuum occasionally, as shall your children for generations to come.*

Enough said.

Ninth commandment: *Change diapers.*

Wiping dirty bottoms is not just women's work! And don't give me that baloney about the smell making you sick. Changing diapers is a learned skill. You were part of your child's creation, so you are responsible for the mess he or she makes. This is all part of nurturing and a big part of respect.

Tenth commandment: *Drive a car pool when and if you can.*

Not only can this be fun, it will also be a learning experience. You will learn a lot from listening to your children interact with others. The conversations you hear or have in the car can be eye-opening, informative, fun, interesting, and even nonsensical at times, and they will also be a source of conversation for you and your wife.

If you are wondering what changing diapers or picking up after yourself or driving a car pool has to do with communication, it is really very simple: this is communication at every level. By doing these things, you communicate to your wife—and to your children for that matter—that your marriage is a partnership. In this day and age when most mothers have to work outside the home, there are no such things as women's chores and men's chores. In this partnership called marriage, you both share duties.

This also helps you understand her day and some of the stress and problems she faces, which will lead to better communication between the two of you. When you share chores, it helps you share and communicate in every other respect as well.

COMMUNICATION TAKES PRACTICE

One night on Johnny Carson's old *Tonight Show* the guest was Jack Lemmon, the actor. During the interview, Jack mentioned that the first year of his married life he was a "kept man." He went to school while his wife worked; she was their sole support. That really connected with me, because I was certainly a kept man the first year of our married life—and I know that is true for many of you.

Isn't it interesting? We never thought twice about the "role reversal" when it involved our getting through med school, law school, graduate school, or starting our businesses. If our wives hadn't kept us, we never would have achieved what we did and gotten our start in life.

Jack Lemmon went on to say that it was one of the happiest years of their married life, and I can say the same. That was a fun, happy time. We shared household duties, we did things together, we communicated.

Communication takes practice. If we quit practicing, we start losing the ability, and this is one of the major things that can happen in a marriage.

If you have a bad day, especially if something significantly stressful happens—perhaps you are at risk of losing your job or of being sued—your wife can read you like a book. If you come home obviously upset and say, when she asks, "No, nothing's wrong," because you are "trying to protect her," you are cutting off communication. Telling her what is wrong will help you deal with the stress and will enable you both to deal with the reality of a situation.

The same is true if you are sick or have a headache. Don't be "afraid to worry her" or think you have to be macho and tough it out. If you consistently refuse to talk about how you feel, either emotionally or physically, it does two things. It establishes a bad communication pattern, and it allows your wife to assume the worst.

While you shouldn't be a whiner or a complainer, you do need to honestly talk with your wife and keep the communication channels open. It is demeaning not to trust her with your true feelings and the truth about what is going on in your life, whether it is physical, mental, emotional, occupational, or social. Relaying facts is important, but communicating your feelings, or at least trying to, will do wonders to avoid that famous lament, "What we have here is a failure to communicate."

We want the ability to communicate, not a failure to communicate.

If you have high school or college-age children at home, you are probably amazed at how long they talk on the phone to their boyfriends and girlfriends. *What are they saying?* you wonder. *What are they talking about???*

We forget, of course, that when we were dating we were the same way. We would talk for hours. Now it takes effort to come up with fifteen minutes a day to talk to each other. Strange, isn't it? When we were dating we didn't hesitate to share our innermost feelings. If we were worried about a test or an interview, we would talk about it. Now we tend not to say anything, even about major concerns.

Unfortunately this failure to communicate, this breakdown in communication, insidiously creeps into many marriages. If this has happened in your marriage, you need to recognize it and make some changes. If you are going to care for the woman you love, if you are to find out how she feels and what her needs are, you have to be able to communicate with her!

CHAPTER
5
All Illnesses
Are Not
Created Equal

Steve and Diane and their three kids decided to go ice skating one afternoon. They were having a grand time when Steve started to get tired and skated over to the side of the ice and sat down on a park bench. While he was resting, he noticed a commotion across the ice and people gathering in one spot. Suddenly someone skated toward him, waving frantically for him to come out on the ice. When he skated over, he discovered Diane lying on the ice in obvious agony, her leg at a grotesque angle.

The paramedics took Diane to the nearest emergency room, where she was told her leg was broken; it was splinted and she was admitted to the hospital. The orthopedic surgeon who saw her late the next day recommended surgery.

Shortly after that, Steve called me for a second opinion, and I agreed to look at the X-rays. When I did, I recommended a different type of surgery. Furthermore, I noticed an ankle fracture that had not been diagnosed.

Steve and Diane requested a transfer to our hospital, where Diane underwent surgery to fix her leg and ankle. The surgery went well, and within six weeks she was walking on the leg in a brace; within three months she was walking on the leg itself. In four months her fractures had healed, and she went on to make a full recovery.

While Diane was immobilized, Steve had to handle the household arrangements and the details of getting the children to and from school. Friends and family were very supportive and pitched in to help when they could. Diane's parents lived in town, so her mother even moved in with them for the first month, enabling Steve to keep his normal work schedule. As a result, there was virtually no interruption in the children's schedule or in Steve's work during the time Diane was recovering.

Diane's rather serious injury was an *acute* illness: that is, an illness or symptom that comes on suddenly and lasts less than three or four months.

All illnesses are not created equal, however; thus, there are many ways to categorize them. Since this isn't a medical textbook, we are going to separate them into four major broad categories: acute, recurring, chronic, and fatal. In subsequent chapters we will then deal with four specific areas that relate to women: PMS and menopause, depression, and breast cancer.

ACUTE ILLNESS

Whether it is a broken leg or pneumonia or appendicitis, the typical acute illness comes on suddenly. When the illness is treated appropriately, healing occurs within a relatively short period of time and full recovery is expected.

Usually couples have no problem agreeing on a treatment plan for such an illness, and mobilizing or managing the household is a temporary inconvenience. Often friends or colleagues or fellow church members are willing to help in an emergency to prevent disruption in work and school schedules, meals, and other everyday needs. I know of many churches who even have special committees to organize help with child care and to bring in meals for a period of time.

With a "we're all in this together and we'll get through it together" attitude, there is no problem mustering support during the limited time of such an illness.

RECURRING OR EPISODIC ILLNESS

Alice and Ted are a striking young couple. Ted is a handsome, extremely bright, hardworking accountant in a large firm. Alice is pretty, peppy, outgoing, and intelligent. At least twice a year Ted's firm holds a major social event to which spouses are invited. There is always one around Christmastime and another whenever the firm takes on a large new account. In the company culture, it is important for the young up-and-comers in the firm to make a good appearance and put their best foot forward at these events.

Unfortunately, Ted and Alice have missed two of the last three of these important events. Both times, baby-sitters were in place, Ted got home on time, they were dressed and driving to the function, when Alice developed a severe migraine headache. The attacks were so bad that she started to vomit. Needless to say, they turned around and went home, and by then it was too late for Ted to go by himself.

Alice suffers with migraine headaches about once every two or three months. Her headaches are very real, *episodic* illnesses. These two just happened to occur on the nights of the firm's events, about nine months apart.

While Ted was concerned for his wife, he also battled feelings of resentment toward her because he feared and expected that these episodes were going to have a negative impact on his career. They did not, however, and this year he will probably become a full partner in the firm.

Marge was an attractive "southern belle" in her late twenties who complained of disabling upper back pains, like a hot poker in her left shoulder blade. When I examined her, I found at least three "trigger points" in her upper back, around the shoulder blade, that were the focus of her symptoms. My diagnosis was tension myalgia or fibromyalgia.

Fibromyalgia is a *recurring* condition, one of its major causes or precipitating factors being physical or emotional stress. This condition is also aggravated by fatigue. The best treatments are massage, back rubs, cold sprays, and aerobic exercise.

After questioning Marge further, I learned she had just moved to the Midwest from the South and that her husband was a youth pastor in a local church. They were now living in a small apartment; down south they'd had a large house. They had not made any friends yet, and her husband was out every night trying to get acquainted with the church young people and their parents.

As a pastor's wife, Marge said, she "couldn't admit to anyone" that she was stressed or having a hard time. This, of course, added to her stress.

The problem with episodic and recurring illness is that the flare-ups never seem to happen at a good time. Almost always, it seems, the illness impacts someone or something adversely. Couple that with the fact that stress frequently plays a role in precipitating the flare-ups and it becomes harder and harder to be sympathetic and caring. Not only is it difficult to be sympathetic, but you can find resentment and even anger building at times because of the suspicion that somehow "she did this on purpose." These conditions can be very trying, and the more often they occur, the more difficult it becomes to deal with them.

CHRONIC ILLNESS

George and Grace were happily married. He was a successful dermatologist and she was a pediatric nurse. One day when Grace was riding horseback a lightning bolt spooked her horse and she was thrown to the ground. She sustained a fractured spine and, over a period of eighteen months, required two major spine surgeries.

Grace now had screws and rods and plates in her back. Her fractures were healed, but she still was plagued with *chronic* pain. Routinely she was taking two or three Tylenol with codeine every three to four hours and had difficulty sleeping through the night. She could no longer play tennis, golf, or ride horseback—all the things she loved and enjoyed. She looked twenty years older than she was, and she stopped seeing all of her friends—or rather they stopped seeing her. They found it increasingly uncomfortable to visit her because all she talked about was her back.

Then George began to have an affair with his office nurse. She was sympathetic to his plight and was someone he could talk to who wasn't complaining all the time.

Eventually George threatened Grace: if she didn't go to a pain clinic and get help, he was going to divorce her. Fortunately she did. She got weaned off her pain medicine and began getting her life back together, although her back still hurt.

George and Grace are still married. He ended the affair, and although Grace had some difficulty dealing with his unfaithfulness, they are working together to try and reestablish their marriage.

George really does love his wife, and he has continued to encourage her in her rehabilitation. While she no longer rides horseback, she has taken up walking and swimming. Also, the two of them can be seen walking together around their neighborhood, and that regular time together has become an important part of both of their days.

Sadly, though, in sharp contrast to Diane and her broken leg, Grace's story is an all-too-common scenario, and many do not end as happily as hers. An acute condition is over in three to four months at the most. A chronic condition usually is incurable, and both husband and wife have to learn to accept and cope with this as a permanent condition — something that is easier said than done.

Those who have suffered with pain or illness for more than three months change psychologically. No matter how stable they are, the pain affects them. This is compounded by medication. Pain medicine, especially codeine, is somewhat addictive; it is also easy to build up a tolerance for it. In other words, the longer you take it, the more you need to get the same effect, so you end up requiring higher and higher doses to get the same amount of pain relief.

There is a saying in medicine that, unfortunately, is true, even though we know much more about pain than ever before: Doctors tend to undertreat acute pain and overtreat chronic pain. Thus, someone who has been hurting for a long time tends to get too much pain medicine, even though both patient and doctor know it isn't working.

THE EMOTIONAL IMPACT OF PAIN

Psychological testing has proven that most people become depressed, hypochondriacal, or hysterical after a few months of chronic pain. Constant pain changes the chemistry in the brain, causing the sufferer to become depressed. And since pain is greater when a person is depressed, this deals a double whammy. Not only does pain medicine not work as well, but the medicine is itself a depressant, making the person hurt "more."

In practical terms, hypochondriacal and hysterical mean that you become more self-centered. People with chronic conditions tend to talk about their illness all the time, because that is what the illness does to them.

If your loved one has been hurting for more than three months, she is likely becoming a different person. She may be irritable, complaining—about everything—depressed, and difficult to live with. (This has nothing to do with hormones; it is true of both men and women.) This change in personality and attitude also has an enormous impact on the support system, for people get very tired of complainers, tired of listening, tired of being sympathetic.

During Diane's relatively short-term injury, everybody pitched in; but with Grace's chronic condition, people gradually got tired and worn out. When an episodic or recurring illness begins to affect others and their plans, it also begins to color their responses. More often than not, people wear down and lose tolerance for those with recurring symptoms and chronic illnesses.

Churches have no trouble mobilizing for a week or two of getting dinner and helping with the children. But when there is no end in sight, it's another story.

Even medical offices and staffs treat the chronic pain sufferer differently.

Most doctors' offices are not geared toward chronic conditions. Chronic pain is, in a sense, the ultimate failure for physicians and nurses, and many aren't prepared to deal with it, either professionally or emotionally; many don't understand it either. Always they seem to offer the unstated or suspected question, "Is the pain real?" Yet even asking the question shows a gross misunderstanding of chronic pain.

Some of this is professional ego: if they can't document it and understand it, then they question whether it's real or "all in the patient's mind."

Ultimately, of course, everything we feel and experience is in our mind, so I am distressed when I hear professionals talk about pain in this way. The bottom line is, some chronic pain is totally incurable and is simply something the person is going to have to live with.

But equally if not more important is the matter of depression and the other emotional effects of pain; addressing all of these things can help mitigate or alleviate a person's suffering. Thus, chronic pain is best addressed in an multidisciplinary pain clinic, where the patient is taught how to manage, adapt to, and live with the pain. This means multiple physicians and psychologists, psychological testing and treatment. The good clinics are quite successful, and they are also expensive. But dealing with your loved one's pain is vital.

Unfortunately, people who suffer chronic pain can at times use that pain to manipulate others. The pain clinic may suggest ways that you should respond to such behavior in order that your behavior does not feed inappropriately into your wife's behavior. Following through on this may be difficult at first and may even seem unloving, but it may be the best thing you can do for your wife. There may even be occasions when you need to ignore certain behaviors or complaints, although this reaction should be reserved for times when the professionals you are consulting have advised you to respond in such a way.

No matter how much you love your wife, what is true of relatives and friends and acquaintances and even physicians is true of you: It gets harder and harder to live with those who are chronically hurting and constantly complaining. They look older, they act older, they are no fun to be around, and they make a lot of extra work for you.

If your wife falls deeper into the trap of chronic pain and begins to change, becoming more and more difficult to live with, your relationship also suffers and changes. This is where sickness and pain can really begin to cause problems in a marriage.

FATAL ILLNESS

Peter and Sonia were the classic American Christian couple. Peter was a successful anesthesiologist and Sonia was very active in her church and other community organizations. Then Sonia noticed a mass in her breast. A mammogram was positive; the biopsy was positive. She had a mastectomy, and the cancer was noted to have spread to the lymph nodes, which put her in a high-risk category.

Sonia underwent radiation and chemotherapy. She lost her hair; then it grew back. She had a recurrence of the cancer and underwent a bone marrow transplant, all within eighteen months.

All of us, her friends, thought the transplant was a hopeless proposition, but five years later Sonia is cured.

Though potentially fatal illnesses may go on for months and years, they tend to have a different psychology and dynamic than recurring or chronic illnesses. When a person is diagnosed with cancer, for example, survival becomes the issue. And rarely do we feel resentment or anger toward the sufferer. Our anger and resentment are more often pointed toward God: Why did He do this to her? Why did He do this to me . . . to us?

In a life-threatening illness, the stresses tend to be spiritual rather than interpersonal, although certainly there can be painful moments within the relationship. Also, the external support of family, friends, and church, especially friends within the church, tends not to slack off as readily, although here, too, it can depend on the individuals involved.

Illnesses are not created equal, and our responses to them are as individual as we are. When they strike, however, we need to deal with them realistically, thoughtfully, and lovingly.

CHAPTER

6

℞ Depression

Mindy was a lovely Christian woman. She and her husband, Mark, were expecting their first child. The pregnancy went fine; the delivery went fine. They had a beautiful baby boy.

When Mindy came home from the hospital, however, something was desperately wrong. She could hardly get out of bed. In fact, she stayed in bed for hours at a time, feeling "blue" and depressed.

Recognizing that something was seriously wrong, Mark sought help for her. With counseling and medication, Mindy's depression lifted. After several months she was off the medication entirely and back to her old self.

Mindy had suffered a severe case of what is commonly called "postpartum blues." (Postpartum means "after delivery.") Usually this is hormonal, and with good reason; dramatic changes occur in a woman after she delivers a baby.

Depression after delivery is a common occurrence and is usually a mild depression that lifts naturally. At times, however, as in Mindy's case, it can be severe, requiring professional help, therapy, and medication.

Megan and Frank had been married for four years, and for three of those years they had been trying to get pregnant. They were in the midst of an extensive "fertility workup and evaluation" when Megan became pregnant. Then, in the fourth month, she miscarried.

Afterward, Megan became severely depressed. Frank would come home at the end of the day and find her still in bed. The church and her friends prayed for her, talked to her, tried to reassure her, all to no avail. Eventually she had to be hospitalized.

Gradually Megan's depression lifted and she became her old self again, but it took several months. Later she was slowly taken off all medication. Within a year she became pregnant again and delivered a healthy baby girl.

While postpartum depression is not rare, it is certainly not the rule; but depression after a miscarriage is the rule rather than the exception.

The medical term for a miscarriage is *abortion;* that is the proper medical term for any pregnancy that ends without a live birth. The medical term for a miscarriage that just happens, as in Megan's case, is *spontaneous abortion.* (Prior to *Roe v. Wade,* abortions performed by an abortionist were *criminal abortions.* Now they are euphemistically called *therapeutic abortions.*)

Regardless of the type, however, the farther along the pregnancy is, the more rapid and devastating the hormonal changes are, and at that point depression is the rule, not the exception. And the farther along the pregnancy, the deeper and more severe the depression when the pregnancy is lost. This is clearly more than grieving over the loss of the pregnancy. The rapid hormonal changes in the woman's body play a significant role in this type of depression.

A sudden dramatic change in hormones can and does lead to depression. While the depression may be predictable, however, the degree and severity and need for treatment vary.

One evening at a church social function I found myself standing next to Gary, and we got talking about what had been happening in our lives recently. He told me that about six months earlier he had come home from work one day and found the two kids running around downstairs and his wife upstairs under the covers, all the blinds pulled; she hadn't been out of bed all day. With hindsight, Gary realized that she had been somewhat down lately, but he had been so busy at work that he had been oblivious. Now, he realized there was a serious problem. At first he was concerned that she might even have had a stroke.

He called a friend to take care of the kids and then took his wife to the emergency room. After checking her out, the doctor ordered emergency psychiatric consultation, and the psychiatrist then suggested that she be hospitalized for acute profound depression.

In less than a week she was back home, and after six months of therapy and medication she was off all medications and doing fine. But, Gary said, the first couple months had been rough.

You remember Gary. He's the young man who was organizing the men's retreat and didn't think there would be much interest in how to cope with a wife who was ill. Needless to say, he now understands.

Mary was a successful swimming coach. Her students loved her, their parents loved her, and many of her swimmers went on to become state champions. But Mary began finding it harder and harder to leave the house and get to practice, harder and harder to go to swim meets. Eventually, much to everyone's surprise, she announced that she was giving up coaching.

Whenever she had to go out of the house, Mary started to breathe fast, she started to get tingling and numbness in her hands and feet, she began sweating profusely and felt sick to her stomach. Then, one day when she had to go out for an appointment, Mary developed chest pain, along with a sensation that she couldn't breathe; her heart was pounding and she was dizzy. She called a neighbor who drove her to the emergency room. Mary spent the evening in the intensive care unit, but all the testing came back normal.

A few weeks later she had a similar episode and once again went to the emergency room. Fortunately the same physician was on duty. He sat down with Mary and her husband and told them that her heart and lungs were fine and that she was having panic attacks. He then recommended that she see a psychiatrist.

Mary's husband was incensed. There had to be something wrong with her heart, he said, and if they couldn't find anything at this hospital, he would take her to another doctor who could find out what the real problem was.

After they got home, Mary and her husband talked it over. The doctor's advice made sense to Mary, so she calmed her husband down and said she would talk to a psychiatrist. He diagnosed agoraphobia—a fear of the outdoors.

Mary responded well to medicine and talk therapy. She still has her moments of fear and terror, but she has gained control over the panic attacks, although she hasn't gotten back into coaching.

Panic attacks are sudden powerful feelings of terror or impending doom. Hallmark symptoms are chest pain, pounding heart, palpitations, a feeling of shortness of breath, a fear of losing control. Frequently the person will begin to hyperventilate and develop numbness and tingling in the hands and feet. In fact the hands and feet may cramp into what are called carpal-pedal spasms so it appears that the person is having some type of seizure. The person can also become nauseated and start to sweat. These symptoms can be very distressing, and it is extremely common for sufferers to end up in the emergency room the first time they occur.

Panic attacks, in varying degrees of severity, are not uncommon, and they can occur in people who are depressed. Counseling from a clinical psychologist or psychiatrist is essential to the treatment of and recovery from recurring bouts of panic attacks.

On the outside it appeared that Joan had everything going for her. She was beautiful, she had been raised in the classic American family, her father was a leading citizen in their hometown, she was married to a successful businessman and had three beautiful children. Yet inside she battled bouts of depression and other physical maladies, none of which were serious but all were troubling to her.

Then Joan's father died. Several months later she became seriously depressed and underwent therapy. During her therapy, terrible memories surfaced. For the first time in her life she confronted and admitted the fact that she had been abused sexually by her father.

Her husband was shocked and appalled; he didn't believe it. He had known his father-in-law well and had liked him. And while he knew his wife had "problems," she had never breathed a word of this to him in the seven years they had been married.

Joan made great strides in therapy, but it took almost a year and a half for her husband to come to grips with the truth and actually believe her. Both of them needed counseling to deal with it.

Sadly, incest and sexual abuse occur in even the "best of families" and even in "Christian families"—much more frequently than most of us can fathom or believe. As in Joan's case, it is very common for the abused person not to be able to come to grips with it or speak of it or even admit it happened until the abusing parent has died. Many times, mood disorders and physical symptoms are really inner manifestations of the turmoil and abuse a person suffered as a child and hasn't faced up to or dealt with or been treated for.

After the death of a parent, "family secrets" often come to light. This is particularly true if the parent has been an alcoholic. His or her death can "free up" the children to face the past.

After the death of my beloved mother-in-law, Lorraine, my wife began to come to grips with her own childhood and the emotional effects that her father's alcoholism had had on her. She had developed profound feelings of fear and insecurity because of the financial and emotional turmoil her dad's drinking had on the whole family, feelings that were generally ignored because of her father's alcoholism.

I had been aware that Judy's father was a reformed alcoholic, but I thought he had been dry and sober since I had known her. He even had an "AA," for Alcoholics Anonymous, tattooed on his arm. When I wrote the first draft of this book, I stated that "he had been dry and sober since I had known her." When Judy read the initial chapters, she was totally blown away by the fact that I thought her father had been dry the whole time I knew her. In fact, he had resumed drinking when she went away to college and he did not attend our wedding because he was drinking and he and her mother were fighting regularly. I didn't know any of this until I began writing this book, which is an example of the "secrets" children raised in alcoholic families learn to keep.

Even though Judy's father had died a number of years before her mother, Judy couldn't come to grips with these issues until her mother died. Judy's therapist told her that it is common for children of alcoholics not to be able to admit or deal with the fact that one or both parents were alcoholics until either one or both parents are dead.

"Being freed" to face such issues, however, can be very stressful in itself, and it is not uncommon for this stress, added to the loss of a parent, to throw the person into a tailspin of depression. This is exactly what happened to my wife.

RECOGNIZING DEPRESSION

I certainly don't want to give you the impression that depression only happens to women or that it is only hormone related. Depression clearly can affect both sexes and it does have a number of causes. What is not clear is why depression is increasing in our culture. Experts believe, with ample evidence, that more people suffer depression than ever before, and that women seem three times as likely as men to become depressed.

Depression falls under the category of conditions commonly called "mood disorders." Certain types of depression are clearly hormone related, such as depression after an abortion, postpartum depression, and the depression associated with menopause. Depression can also be a cyclic disorder, or what is called manic-depressive disorder, where the person fluctuates between a hyperkinetic or manic phase and a severe depression.

By depression we do not mean just "feeling down" or "feeling a little blue." Almost all of us, at some point, will feel that way. But those are times when we can "snap out of it" with exercise or a long walk in the woods or a positive word from someone or even a nice long soak in a hot tub.

Depression, on the other hand, is a "real downer." The old-fashioned term was melancholia—a persistent sadness, emptiness, or anxiousness. Its victims feel truly hopeless and worthless.

Sufferers of depression lose their interest in pleasurable activity, in sporting activities and exercise, and they lose all sexual desire. In severe depression people become almost immobilized and may spend days in bed. They feel worthless and lose interest in life itself. This sense of hopelessness may be one of the reasons depression is one of the major causes of suicide.

While depressed people feel very tired, even exhausted, and do not have energy to do anything, they also have difficulty sleeping. In the morning, however, they have trouble getting out of bed, even though they may not be sleepy.

Some depressed people lose their appetite and their interest in food and, consequently, lose weight. Some do just the opposite; they gain weight when they are depressed because, even though they are not really hungry, they eat more. For many women, this weight gain is a depressing event piling on top of depression. The more weight they gain, the more depressed they become.

Depressed people cannot concentrate well and tend to be forgetful. They also have enormous difficulty making decisions, regardless of how minor those decisions might be. They are moody and irritable; they cry easily and for no apparent reason. Typically, depressed people have recurring thoughts of death or suicide.

Physical symptoms become magnified when a person is depressed. Headaches, digestive disorders, constipation, cramping, diarrhea, nausea, and just not feeling well are all symptoms and signs of depression. Any painful existing conditions are magnified by depression, and, as we discussed earlier, any chronic condition that has gone on for more than three months will lead to some kind of depression, magnifying those symptoms. Even normal bodily functions can be magnified into symptoms when someone is depressed.

Depression can be precipitated by the loss of a loved one—a parent or child, a brother or sister or friend. At times, however, depression just seems to come out of the blue, with no accountable cause. People who have "everything going for them" and seem "to have the world by the tail" can become depressed. Those of us on the outside looking in can't see any obvious reason why they would become depressed.

WHAT SHOULD I DO?

If you think your wife is depressed or know she is, the first thing you need to do is address the matter openly and honestly: "Honey, I think you are depressed or down about something." You need to get her to talk about it and admit to it.

I can tell you from personal experience that one of the hardest things to do is to tell a loved one, especially your wife, that she is depressed. The more you love her, the more difficult it is. Deep down you have this nagging fear that something is wrong, but you are afraid that what you are going to tell her is going to make her worse, or you are going to hurt her feelings, or she is going to get angry and deny it, and then what do you do? Yet telling her is the most loving, caring thing you can do.

There is no cookbook way to do it, but it is best to confront it head-on: "There is something wrong. You are not yourself. You seem down (or, you seem depressed, or, you are depressed)."

Ideally, she will acknowledge it and say, "Yes, I know, and I'm struggling with it," or some such thing, which is a good sign. Typically, however, she may deny it, especially if you are convinced that things are bad enough that she needs therapy or treatment. She may refuse to seek treatment. She can be so depressed that she is too depressed to seek treatment when that is the very thing she needs.

If she denies that there is anything wrong or that she is depressed, another tactful way to handle it is to express your concern by saying, "Honey, I'm worried about you. You have to go see the doctor and have them check your blood count. Maybe you have the flu or are anemic or something."

Prior to that appointment, you should communicate your fears or concerns to her physician, along with your willingness to accept a diagnosis of depression or other mood disorder and your assurance that you will seek any help that is indicated. You can either call and talk to the physician before your wife's appointment or arrange to see the physician outside the presence of your wife before the consultation. (If you insist on a doctor's evaluation to help convince your wife of the need for treatment, you must go to that consultation with her.) Ironically, many physicians struggle just as you are struggling in confronting family and patients with the fact that the problem isn't an organic illness but is a mood disorder. If your wife's doctor realizes your willingness to accept the diagnosis, that can aid significantly in being able to address the issue with you and your wife.

However, your willingness and support are not enough. Your wife must accept the fact that she is depressed and needs help, and then she must be willing to seek help. So you need to be open, express your concerns to her, and encourage her to seek medical help from either your family doctor or a psychiatrist. Depression is nothing to be ashamed of; it is more common than diabetes. It is, in fact, an epidemic that is sweeping our country.

If the depression is mild, you can help your wife a great deal by getting her to exercise with you. Any type of aerobic exercise—bicycling, walking, jogging, or swimming—helps lift depression because of the changes in brain chemistry that occur with such exercise. So any type of activity or aerobic exercise can be very therapeutic.

If your wife is profoundly depressed—that is, she is hiding under the covers, bedridden, or just not functioning—then you may need to have her hospitalized. You will need the help of your family physician or psychiatrist to decide this, and I would strongly recommend that you follow their advice if they recommend hospitalization.

If your wife does not respond to treatment while she is hospitalized, her psychiatrist may even recommend electroshock therapy. There is some controversy surrounding this therapy, and certainly fifteen years or more ago it was a barbaric form of treatment. But the way it is done now in modern psychiatric institutions is safe and can be very effective if nothing else is working. So if this is suggested, you need to openly discuss it with your wife's physician; it may be the best thing that can be done for her.

Treatment for depression has been one of the great triumphs of medicine. Regardless of the type or the cause, most depression can be treated successfully. The treatment usually is a combination of talk therapy and medicine. People who are depressed have brains that chemically are working differently and are deficient in certain chemicals. These imbalances can be remedied with modern antidepressant medicines. Such medicine works just like antibiotics work for infection and can be essential for full recovery.

IS DEPRESSON A PUNISHMENT?

Over twenty years ago one of the great American psychiatrists, Dr. Karl Menninger, wrote a book that posed a question to our culture, *Whatever Became of Sin?* Certainly nothing in the past twenty years has changed the validity of that question. If anything, it is more pertinent than ever.

The Bible says that incest, drunkenness (alcoholism), adultery, jealousy, lying, cheating, greed, and gluttony are all sins. Yet many scoff at that word. All we hear is "positive reinforcement" and "affirmation" to make us "feel good."

Karl Menninger believed that one of the underlying problems behind the epidemic rise in mood disorders and mental illness was unresolved sin and the consequences of sin. Certainly children who are victims of incest or who have been raised by alcoholic parents are suffering for "the sins of the fathers and mothers."

Furthermore, mental illness and mood disorders do affect our relationship with God. When we feel worthless, we feel worthless before God as well. We lose interest in spiritual things, we lose interest in church life, and we feel abandoned by God.

The psalmist David cried out in his depression, "God, where are you?"

Save me, O God,
for the waters have come up to my neck.
I sink in the miry depths,
where there is no foothold.
I have come into the deep waters;
the floods engulf me.
I am worn out calling for help;
my throat is parched.
My eyes fail,
looking for my God.
—Psalm 69:1–3

While I firmly believe that sin can and does cause certain physical, emotional, and mood symptoms, that is different than saying all mood disorders and all physical illnesses are punishment for sin or the result of unresolved or unconfessed sin. I do not believe that at all! Nor does the Bible imply or say that. In fact, it states the opposite, as we will discuss in the next chapter.

My hope and prayer is that you never have to face the issue of depression in your family or among your friends. Unfortunately, it is likely that you will, since depression is an all too common problem that is becoming more frequent.

We all have to be more sensitive to the feelings and moods of our loved ones and coworkers because most of us are either going to battle depression ourselves or relate to loved ones or friends or acquaintances who are depressed. Even though the depressed person may feel hopeless and worthless, it is important that we not be judgmental and think that somehow he or she is weak or undeserving or being punished by God. This can be a very destructive reaction and can significantly affect your relationship with the person who is depressed.

Chapter 6

While it is not absolutely accurate, you might try looking at depression the same way you would look at pneumonia. The person who has pneumonia is seriously ill with a disease that if not addressed and treated can be crippling or even fatal; but with appropriate antibiotics, pneumonia usually responds very well to treatment. With appropriate medication and other treatment, depression can be treated quite successfully as well.

CHAPTER

7

PMS and
Menopause

Tanya was a happily married thirty-three-year-old woman. She had two lovely children, and her husband, Al, was a hardworking executive for a Christian missions organization. Tanya had been raised in a strict fundamentalist Christian home where women were taught that their primary goal in life was to please their husbands and thus serve God.

Tanya struggled mightily with this mandate one week a month, however, when she would be angry for several days and then depressed for several days, and then have her period and be fine. She thought she had been able to hide this from her husband, and she had prayed about it, "giving her concerns over to the Lord," and had even read a book on how to have a Spirit-filled temperament. Until the day she got so angry with what she read that she tried to throw the book through a wall!

It was a hot July day in the Midwest, and Tanya and Al had planned to leave on a week's vacation at one o'clock. Al promised he'd be home by twelve.

One o'clock rolled around, and there was no Al. The little girls began worrying that they wouldn't be able to go on vacation if Daddy was late. Two o'clock, three o'clock . . . . Finally at four-thirty Al came home, offered a brief apology, and said, "Okay, let's get going."

While walking through the kitchen, he noticed something on the floor and said something to the effect that "We can't leave a dirty kitchen floor. It will draw ants while we're gone."

For the first time in her married life, Tanya "lost it." She grabbed the broom out of the closet, started sweeping, broke the leg off a chair in the process, and grew white-hot with anger. She started screaming at Al about how he was the one who was late and was ruining the kid's vacation. She felt terrible.

They left for vacation that night as Tanya was finally calming down. Later, trying to get to sleep, she could feel herself sinking into a depression. She felt that way for the next two days; then she had her period and felt fine for the rest of their vacation.

Three weeks later, the anger started to rise again. It took all her will and fortitude to keep from screaming at the kids and Al. Then it clicked. This was four days before her period again.

She called her gynecologist. She demanded to speak to the doctor and got extremely angry on the phone until the office nurse finally put her through to him.

"Hey, Tanya, how are you doing?" Steve said.

She almost bit his head off through the phone. "I can't stand who I am. I can't stand the way I am. You have got to do something. You have got to give me something."

Steve tried to calm her down. "Now, Tanya, don't tell me you've just been reading that latest medical journal *Cosmopolitan*?"

"No, I haven't and I need to see you," she screamed.

"Okay, okay," he said, "I'll get the nurse back on the phone and we'll get a time when you can come in."

When Tanya got to Steve's office, she broke down in tears as she told him she just couldn't stand living on this emotional seesaw.

After listening to her explanation, Steve told her that she was experiencing severe premenstrual syndrome and that there was relief for it. Because her symptoms were so severe, he said, he wanted her to get a calendar solely for her own use. On it she would keep track of her monthly cycle. On those days when she felt angry and upset, she should put a large red dot. On those days when the curtain came down and she felt depressed, she should put a blue dot. On those days when she had her period, she should put a green dot. On those days when she felt fine, she would put whatever other color she chose to signify that was a good day for her.

"That's the way we're going to monitor how you feel," Steve said. "And on the red dot and blue dot days, you'll take Provera."

Tanya now says it was like a miracle. Provera changed her life.

Interestingly enough, fifteen years later her daughter, Kerry, called her one day from college, depressed and crying. Something clicked, and Tanya said, "Is it four days until your period?"

At first there was silence at the other end of the line. Then Kerry said, "How did you know that?"

Tanya immediately arranged for her daughter to see a gynecologist at the women's clinic at the medical school of the university she was attending. Because Kerry had severe PMS symptoms, she was put on Aldactone, a diuretic, plus birth control pills and a progesterone supplement to help control the symptoms.

Four months later Kerry's fiancé drove sixty miles to the women's clinic to thank the gynecologist who treated her because, "You gave me back the woman I love." He then related how one week a month Kerry had been so impossible that he had started to question their relationship because of the way she behaved. Now that she was under treatment, she was an entirely different woman.

PMS

Contrary to the material of many stand-up comedians, PMS is not a joke. It is very real, and it isn't a laughing matter. Yet with all our modern advances in medicine, the science or physiology behind premenstrual syndrome is still poorly understood. Nor do we know why some women are more susceptible than others. Clearly, hormones and fluid retention play a role, but the exact cause is still to be determined.

PMS is hormonal because it is cyclical and "monthly." In addition to this, the best explanation seems to be that during the fluid retention that occurs in the days immediately before the onset of the menstrual period there may be some fluid retention in the brain which accounts for the irritability and moodiness that is typical of PMS.

Some recent research has shown that Prozac, the famous antidepressant drug, can be effective in alleviating the symptoms of PMS in about half of the women who suffer from severe symptoms. The theory behind this is that the chemical serotonin is lacking in the brain and the Prozac helps remedy that imbalance. The classic treatments for PMS, however, are high protein diets, no caffeine, regular exercise, and vitamin B.

Supposedly only about 8 percent of women, or one in twelve, suffer these severe symptoms, but over 40 percent have some symptoms of PMS. At least that is what the medical literature says. Women themselves lean more toward the 40 percent.

Women who suffer from PMS certainly know that they do, but they are not always aware of their obvious, and often obnoxious, behavioral changes. This can be stressful for both husband and wife. If her symptoms are severe and you can't stand her on those days, she needs to know this. That's why it is so important that you communicate with each other regularly. Otherwise you may find yourselves screaming at each other and not communicating at all. That can be very destructive and you don't want that to happen.

If your wife is suffering from these symptoms and it is a red dot day, my best advice is to get out of the way. If it is a blue dot day, try to get her to exercise with you. Ideally, your wife should be keeping a calendar just as Tanya did, but if she won't, you should start doing it; when she sees you doing this, she may realize that what she is experiencing fits a very predictable cycle. Then, using the calendar as a guide, she needs to talk with her gynecologist or family physician.

MENOPAUSE

Donna was a happily married mother of four. Then, at forty-three, she had to have a hysterectomy. After the surgery, however, this woman who had been emotionally stable all her life suddenly became irritable, nervous, jumpy, had hot flashes, and was no longer interested in sex at all. Since Donna and her husband had had an excellent sex life prior to the surgeries, he knew something was desperately wrong.

Donna herself felt she was coming apart at the seams and that her marriage was deteriorating. When she tried to talk to her doctor, he did not seem very interested or helpful. He thought she was just depressed and run-down from the surgery. Donna, an extremely bright woman with a Ph.D. in literature, began to study and read about depression and finally convinced her doctor to prescribe some hormones. He prescribed Premarin as estrogen hormone replacement therapy. She improved somewhat but still was having a lot of difficulty.

After her doctor recommended that she see a psychiatrist, Donna began to make a daily chart of her moods while she extensively researched female hormones and hormone replacement therapy. As a result, she convinced her doctor to try Estrace, the other commonly prescribed estrogen replacement hormone. Within a month's time she was a different woman. She was back on her even keel, her marriage had improved dramatically, and she was no longer short and cross with the kids. Her life had been turned around.

Although her hysterectomy plunged her into menopause early, what happened to Donna is not untypical of women in menopause. Every woman goes through menopause, and over 75 percent of all women develop significant disabling symptoms during that time.

Common symptoms are moodiness, irritability, and unpredictability. Women suffering such symptoms may lose their temper over the slightest thing or scream at the kids. They may suddenly be overwhelmed with "hot flashes," which means they break out in a sweat—even in a cold room. They may lower the thermostat in the dead of winter, even open windows when it is below freezing outside.

Women in menopause can become depressed, mildly to severely. They can develop heart palpitations, have trouble sleeping, have dry, itchy, or tingly skin, and become anxious and forgetful. They may lose interest in any sexual activity. Part of this is psychological, but some may be physical. The size of the vagina may start to shrink and the lining may dry out and lose its lubricant; thus, it hurts to have intercourse.

In fact, the books on menopause written by women for women say that at least 70 percent of the women with these symptoms sometimes are "not fit to live with."

On the average, when a woman is in her mid-forties her ovaries begin to stop producing the female hormone estrogen. (Menopause can start as early as thirty-five and go to the mid-fifties.) As the estrogen level falls, all of the symptoms we have described above can and do occur in most women. (A fortunate 25 percent have no ill effects at all.)

As the estrogen level falls, its protective effect against heart disease no longer is present, so women start catching up with men in heart disease and hardening of the arteries. Their skin dries out and they become wrinkled. Also, their bones start to soften as they begin losing calcium content. Over a period of ten to twenty years without estrogen, women's bones become soft and start to collapse. This is the reason many elderly women seem to be bent over with humpbacks. Their spines have started to collapse and literally become C-shaped. Also, their hips become more fragile, which is the reason elderly women tend to get hip fractures. All because their bodies have stopped making the essential female hormone estrogen.

Most gynecologists use the cessation of hot flashes as the criterion for the proper doses of estrogen, but hot flashes stop at approximately an estradiol level of twenty. I have a good friend who is an obstetrician gynecologist, and his wife's estradiol level was twenty. One day she bent over while gardening and suffered a spinal fracture. That simple movement had caused the injury because she was developing osteoporosis. Her husband now believes that the ideal estradiol level in women on hormone replacement therapy is eighty—four times the level that normally stops hot flashes. His wife's estradiol level is now at two hundred because of the osteoporosis she developed in her late forties.

Actually, menopause is a misnomer. Menopause literally means "pause in menstrual period." But there is no pause; it is a permanent change. It should be called menostop. However, the estrogen doesn't just stop cold turkey. There is an ebb and flow in the estrogen level, which accounts for the mood swings and the hot flashes.

Many, if not all, of these disabling symptoms can be treated and minimized with hormone replacement therapy. The primary female hormone is estrogen, and there is a secondary female hormone called progesterone.

For decades the only hormone replacement was a drug called Premarin. It has worked well and has been a safe and effective treatment for many women. Recently, however, chemists have been able to synthesize estradiol, the naturally occurring substance in the body that becomes estrogen. Estradiol can be taken by the mouth in the form of Estrace or by using a skin patch.

The most commonly prescribed medication is Premarin. It has been around the longest, so most gynecologists and physicians have more experience with it. But if your wife is not doing well on Premarin, either the dosage is too low or she is not tolerating it. If that is the case, then she should

definitely try the estradiol or Estrace. (This is not a recommendation I make lightly, and it is a recommendation I made
to both my wife and my sister; in fact, Donna, whom I
mentioned above, was the first person to make this recommendation to me.)

The problem is, absolutely no research has been done on
the mood effect differences, if any, between Premarin and
Estrace. It is important, therefore, for your wife to keep a
daily diary of her moods and medications, because there is
no question that the different hormones can cause subtle and
sometimes not-so-subtle differences in moods and emotions.

The other fact you need to know about estrogen replacement therapy is that estrogen stimulates the lining of the
uterus to get thicker. When it does, it may cause spotting, an
unpleasant side effect. Because of this, a different hormone,
progesterone, will frequently be prescribed. In fact, many
gynecologists recommend cycling estrogen and progesterone, on a cycle similar to the menstrual cycle. This, they
believe, decreases if not eliminates the risk of cancer of the
uterus. By stopping the estrogen and increasing the level of
progesterone, the lining of the uterus that was stimulated by
the estrogen is then stimulated to "slough off" the excess
lining. This is healthy and is thought by many to be added
insurance against any possible carcinogenic effects of the
estrogen. This cycling is virtually the same type of cycling
created by birth control pills and will cause a monthly
period. But progesterone is a different hormone, and it does
have different mood and emotional effects than estrogen.

I say all this because you need to be aware of the effects
and side effects of the hormones your wife may be taking.
Your wife's doctor is likely only going to look at her physical
signs and symptoms: how dry and tender is her vagina, how
many hot flashes and hot sweats has she had, how itchy is

her skin, how much bleeding and spotting is she having? For the most part, that is all doctors will use in deciding the dosage of hormones to prescribe. Their training and textbooks tend to ignore or minimize the emotional symptoms and signs of depression. To a certain extent that is understandable, because it is very difficult to measure emotion, depression, and mood. It is just not as "scientific." Yet that is where the "art" of medicine comes into play. A good physician will be sensitive to this. However, the physician sees your wife a few times a year, at most, and in an office setting. So he or she must rely on information given by your wife.

That is why you and your wife have to communicate with each other. You must validate the way she is feeling. If she is down, you must tell her. If she is jumpy or edgy, you must tell her. Not in a nagging way, but informing her—letting her know she is not "going crazy," that she is different today than she was yesterday. She is not imagining things.

Almost everyone in medicine and women who have researched the subject agree that it is better to take hormone replacement therapy than to endure the symptoms of menopause. Furthermore, the complications of low estrogen are very disabling, especially osteoporosis and cardiovascular or heart problems.

What are the risks of taking hormone replacement therapy? First, it can reinstitute menstrual periods. While this is not a great risk, it is a great nuisance. Second, the patches sometimes cause skin rashes. This is usually just a localized and minor irritant, but it is enough to make many women stop using the patches. Third, and of greatest concern to many women—and cause of much recent controversy on the subject—there is the possibility of an increased risk of breast cancer.

Certain types of breast cancer are sensitive to estrogen, and for that reason, some women, particularly those who have either had breast cancer or who have a history of it in their family, cannot take estrogen replacement therapy. However, most of the experts agree that if there is a risk, it is slight, and is usually far outweighed by all the other positives that occur from taking hormone replacement therapy. Risks of dying of heart disease, stroke, or complications of hip fractures are far greater than the slight statistical risk of breast cancer as a result of hormone replacement therapy.

I know some people argue that it is not natural to take hormone replacement therapy. These same arguments could be applied to diabetes. People are diabetic because their bodies do not produce enough insulin, a hormone that controls blood sugar. When this happens, many horrendous symptoms and medical complications occur, including blindness, nerve inflammation and neuralgia, glaucoma, strokes, heart attacks, and death. All because the body isn't making enough of the hormone insulin. Yet I don't ever recall anyone arguing that a diabetic should not take insulin because it is not natural. Taking insulin alleviates a lot of pain and suffering. So does hormone replacement therapy.

For the most part, hormone replacement therapy is a simple treatment, and the positive results and benefits are felt very quickly and very predictably. Your wife will be a happier, healthier person because of it.

WHEN HER DISCOMFORT BECOMES YOURS

Female hormones do affect mood, and depression is one of the common symptoms of menopause. But how can you tell whether the depression is solely the result of insufficient hormones? In other words, if a woman is depressed and then becomes menopausal, how do you tell what part of the depression is caused by menopause and what part is due to other causes?

Your best option, of course, would be to have your wife consult both her physician and a psychiatrist and then ask the two to consult and compare notes regarding her treatment. While this seems eminently logical, don't expect it to happen. Unfortunately, gynecologists and psychiatrists rarely, if ever, compare notes on a patient. Therefore, your wife, with your support, is going to have to take charge in asking for adjustments in her hormones or her antidepressant medication.

To do this she must keep a diary and a calendar. If she is depressed, however, you may have to encourage her to fill out this daily diary, recording what medication she is taking (both hormones and antidepressant medications), what dosages, any physical symptoms she might have, and how she feels (her emotional state). If she doesn't take charge and command of her treatment and doesn't keep track of her mood swings and doses of medications, she is likely to have problems. For this reason, good psychiatrists and gynecologists encourage women to keep diaries. She is going to need your support with this, and she will need your input to reinforce her own opinion and validate her own feelings.about herself.

Get a calendar with plenty of room to write for each day of the month. On the days she is angry and upset, use a red dot or X. On the days she is down or depressed, put a blue dot or X. On the days she is spotting or having a menstrual flow, put a green dot or X. On the days when she is feeling fine, use another color to mark a dot or an X. In addition to these color codes, every day she must record the medications or hormones and dosage that she has taken. She should then take these monthly records when she goes to the doctor.

The treatment of a depressed menopausal woman can be tricky and difficult. And while this stage of life can be frustrating and depressing for your wife, it can also be frustrating and depressing for you.

> For this reason a man will leave his father and mother and be united to his wife, and they will become *one flesh*. (Genesis 2:24, italics added)

The concept of "one flesh" is deep, profound, and mystical, but there is no question that in marriage you are uniquely united. When one of you is suffering, it affects both of you. Her discomfort becomes your discomfort. Her mood changes affect you, and your responses affect her. You can aggravate the problem, or you can grow through it together.

Symptoms of menopause, as well as PMS, can seriously affect your relationship and can be destructive for your marriage. The physical changes, the emotional changes, and the sexual changes your wife experiences will impact both of you. This can be a devastating time in your marriage, or it can be a time when your relationship grows and deepens as you show your love for her and work through this together. By doing this, you will understand her better and you will have communicated to her your true love for her. She will feel more secure because of your faithfulness in this, and your marriage will grow deeper and richer.

You truly will become "one flesh." And you will honor God by doing so.

CHAPTER
8

Choosing a Doctor

It is a frightening statistic: One out of every nine women in the United States will face breast cancer at some point during her lifetime. The suggestions I am going to make regarding breast cancer, however, really apply to any disabling, potentially crippling, or potentially fatal illness.

A diagnosis of breast cancer (or of any potentially fatal or crippling condition) is terrifying to anyone at any time. It is an enormous shock to your wife, to you, to your whole family, and this is one of those times when you must become involved in treatment and treatment procedures regarding your wife. (I said you should be *involved*, not that you should make all the decisions!)

The first step is going to key consultations with the doctor where diagnosis and treatment are discussed. By doing this, you demonstrate to your wife that you care for her. It is also important that you know what the potentially life-threatening decisions are. If the treatment is unsuccessful or you choose the wrong treatment plan or you don't treat the illness, your decision can be fatal. And finally, if the diagnosis is a major one, such as "cancer," once your wife hears those words, she may hear nothing else that is said.

Research shows that patients hear only ten to thirty percent of what their doctors tell them. So no matter how bright or well-educated your wife is, at least two-thirds of what her doctor tells her may not even register. Thus, you need to be there not only for encouragement, but to help listen to what is said and to help her decide on the treatment plan the doctor prescribes.

To do this, you need to get the facts. If you have trouble remembering, then take notes. Actually, that's probably good advice for everyone, because you're under stress in this situation too, and nobody's memory is infallible.

CRITICAL DECISIONS AND GUIDELINES

Dealing with a serious illness like cancer means you will be making many decisions—critical decisions. The first of these has to do with your doctor. *Does your wife trust her doctor? Do you trust her doctor?* It is more essential that she trust her doctor, but in a sense you both should. If you don't, your wife needs to know that you don't and why. If, after discussing your reservations or concerns, your wife still has a great deal of faith in this doctor and wants to continue with him or her, I suggest that you honor her decision.

The second equally important decision is really intertwined with the first: *How well does your doctor communicate?*

Does he or she communicate well with your wife? Does he or she communicate well with you? It is one thing to trust doctors, but it is another thing to be able to communicate with and fully understand them. If you really can't communicate with your wife's doctor, then I suggest that you change doctors. If your wife can communicate with the doctor and you can't, then the two of you need to discuss it. Again, the communication between your wife and her doctor is paramount, but a good doctor should be able to communicate with both of you.

Trust and communication are key. If you can't communicate with and you can't trust a particular doctor, there is no point in going any further with him or her. If your wife does not trust her doctor, she is not going to get better.

The third issue is a tough one. *How good is the doctor your wife is seeing?*

Here are several guidelines you can use. First of all, when you or your wife make the appointment for a consultation, ask if the doctor is board certified or board eligible. Board certification means a doctor has completed an advanced residency program in his or her specialty. In fact this even applies to family practitioners. Today, there is a board certification in emergency room medicine, family practice, and every other area of medicine.

There are a couple exceptions here. Some experienced and excellent doctors, especially family practitioners, began practicing long before family practice boards were available, so they are one possible exception to the rule of board certification. The other exceptions are young doctors who, while highly trained and highly competent, have not been in practice long enough to sit for the examination. So they would not be board certified, but they should be board eligible!

The second way to determine your doctor's qualifications is to ask about his or her experience, including experience treating those with your wife's condition—whether it is migraine headaches, fibromyalgia, or breast cancer. If the doctor treats hundreds or even thousands of cases a year, then you know you are dealing with an experienced physician or surgeon. Conversely, if your wife is only the second or third person the doctor has seen with this condition, then this may not be the physician who should be treating your wife.

This may depend, of course, on how rare your wife's condition is. There are some conditions that even the most experienced doctors have seen only two or three times in their career.

Be aware that while some doctors are not threatened by being asked to verify their experience, others may be. You might want to reconsider any doctor who seems uncomfortable with this question or who becomes defensive.

The last consideration in choosing a doctor may or may not be an issue for you: Is he or she a Christian? Some Christians are more comfortable being treated by Christian physicians, and if you or your wife have more faith and trust in a Christian physician, then that is a legitimate issue. Certainly I believe it plays an important role when you are dealing with a terminal condition—when the end-of-life issues and life support come into play. In that circumstance, having a Christian physician who sympathizes with your views can be very important.

If you are not in that type of situation, however, my own view is that it is more important to have a competent and experienced physician you trust than to go to a less experienced and possibly less competent physician simply because he or she is a Christian.

Your wife's faith—and yours—is more important than the physician's faith. Also, in certain areas of specialty there simply may not be any Christian physicians available to you, or the non-Christian physician may be more qualified than the Christian physician.

CRUCIAL QUESTIONS

Once you have determined the doctor to treat your wife's condition, there are several questions you must ask him or her. Again, if you are someone who is going to forget in the stressful situation of the doctor's consultation room, then write these questions down ahead of time and bring a pad and pencil so you can take notes.

First Question: *What happens if there is no treatment?*

Obviously in many cases, such as breast cancer, if the condition is not treated, it will most likely kill your wife, although there are exceptions.

Tammy is a slim, fit woman who looks at least ten years younger than her forty-three years. She leads a vigorous, active lifestyle and is very knowledgeable medically. About ten years ago she learned that she had a fibrocystic disease of the breast, meaning that she had multiple lumps and cysts in her breasts that made palpitation and self-examination very difficult. After that, over a period of time, she had four breast biopsies, all negative. The fifth one, however, came back with a diagnosis of cancer. Tammy consulted three doctors, and all agreed that the cancer was such a type and the biopsy was so well done that no further treatment was necessary at that point in her life.

There are some conditions where life and death are not the issue. And there are some conditions where the cure is worse than the disease. So the first legitimate question, whatever the disease, is what happens if it is not treated? Is this a progressive disease? Will crippling or death occur? Will increasing pain occur? Could my wife get better without treatment? What are the chances of that happening?

Second Question: *What happens if the treatment is successful?*

Mary was an aerobic dance instructor who had developed an arthritic hip. The hip had become so painful that she could no longer teach aerobics five days a week. She could bicycle, swim, or walk comfortably, but she wanted to continue to teach aerobics. Her doctor recommended hip replacement surgery, and she came to me for a second opinion. I concurred that she did have a mildly arthritic hip, but that hip replacement would not solve her problem. High impact aerobics is not recommended for anybody who has an artificial hip joint (regardless of what Bo Jackson did).

Once Mary learned that, even with a successful operation, she would not be able to teach aerobics, she was more than happy to accept her disability and forego extensive hip surgery at her relatively young age. She could actually do aerobics once or twice a week, but her hip would get sore. When she realized she could be relatively pain-free by eliminating impact-type activities such as running and aerobics, she decided to stick with swimming and bicycling and cross-country skiing to try and "preserve" her hip as long as she could and thus delay the need for artificial hip replacement.

A more tragic example is Jennifer, mother of four. Jennifer had smoked all her life and at age forty-four developed severe tongue and throat cancer. It had spread extensively and a radical surgery called a commando or "Andy Gump" operation was recommended. Jennifer's doctors told her that even with the surgery her chances of cure were no better than ten or fifteen percent; without surgery, they were five to eight percent. The problem was that with "successful surgery" Jennifer would lose half of her jaw, her voice box, and her tongue. Once she saw several people on the cancer ward who'd had these operations, saw and heard the results of this surgery, she elected to have the nonsurgical radiation and chemotherapy treatment, even though it was statistically less likely to be a success. Since her chance of cure was not good with either one and the cancer had spread already, she did not want her children to remember her as a horribly disfigured person.

Third Question: *What are the chances of success of the treatment?*

Whether the treatment is medical, chemotherapy, surgery, or no treatment, an informed doctor knows the statistical chances of good results.

In the case of breast cancer, for example, the chances of successful treatment vary tremendously according to the type of cancer, location in the breast, how advanced the cancer is at the time diagnosed, the cell characteristics, and the age of the woman. Also, with certain types of breast cancer, the surgeon may recommend that the noninvolved breast be excised as well.

Chance of successful treatment also varies with surgery. Surgery can be radical or simple, surgery can be done with or without chemotherapy, chemotherapy can be given during or immediately after surgery, and of course there is radiation therapy. Many new agents are available for specific cancers. And there is bone marrow transplantation. For many tumors, bone marrow transplantation is the chemotherapy of last resort. Any cancer specialist experienced enough in doing bone marrow transplantation knows the statistical chances of success.

As you can see, these are very serious decisions, and you need to be there with your wife at these times. In the case of breast cancer, your wife is thinking not only of the life-threatening diagnosis; she is also thinking of what it will mean to have one or no breasts—the effect that will have on her appearance and your relationship. She is worried that her appearance will turn you off or, worse yet, that you may leave her. You have got to be there for her at these times.

Our culture has been rightly criticized as being overly enamored with the female breast. One cannot pick up a sports magazine, or watch TV, or look at a book rack without seeing how valid that criticism is. Our society is fascinated with and fixated on the female breast. This fascination, however illogical, is involved in all the emotional agony that your wife is undergoing at this time. Be there to support her, reassure her, and love her. Your support and caring will improve the chances of success of any treatment she has, and it will bring you closer together.

A loving, caring family aids in the treatment and recovery of many illnesses.

Fourth Question: *What are the potential complications, and what are the chances of these potential complications?*

Some medications are safer than aspirin; others can cause severe complications. Some types of chemotherapy, for example, have a significant risk of permanently damaging the heart.

Some operations are safer than the automobile drive to the hospital; some are not. Most surgeons get a bit sweaty-palmed when you ask about potential complications, and if you ask for a list of every complication, you and your wife will be horrified.

For this reason, I believe a better way to ask the question is, "Doc, what are the complications we realistically have to worry about? We are willing to accept that there are always certain risks with surgery and certain risks with anesthesia, but what are the complications that would realistically happen with this type of surgery you are proposing, and what do you see as the chances of these happening—1 percent or 30 percent?"

For example, as I write this, the risk of bone marrow transplant mortality is 10 percent. That means there is a one in ten chance that the treatment will kill the recipient. Realistically you want to know about complications that are more common than 1 or 2 percent. You certainly want to know about any risk of complication that is 10 percent or higher.

Fifth Question: *How soon must we get on with this treatment or surgery?*

Obviously if your wife has appendicitis, you don't have a week or a month to make up your mind. You need to make the decision now! However, there are instances where people feel pressure to make a decision when leisurely contemplation is in order. So don't hesitate to ask this question. Very few conditions require surgery in less than a week's time.

Sixth Question: Actually, this is a two-part question.

First, ask your physician or surgeon: *What would you do if this were your wife or husband? What would you do if this were your colleague's spouse?*

And second, ask: *Doc, do I need to get a second opinion?*

The first question is pretty straightforward. The issue of second opinions is a bit more difficult.

I do not know a competent physician who is offended by this question. If your physician does become offended and upset, then maybe you really do need a second opinion!

When I am asked that question, I often say "yes," or I might even recommend it before the patient brings up the subject. But there are times when I reply that a second opinion may only confuse the issue. It doesn't happen often, but sometimes a second opinion can be counterproductive.

If your doctor suggests that you get a second opinion, then, in my opinion, you should get one. If your doctor seems confused and if your wife does not respond to the treatment the way she should be responding, then I think you should get a second opinion.

When Maria came back from a trip to Central America, she was running a fever and had swollen joints. She saw her family physician, who also sent her to a specialist on infectious diseases. The two physicians decided that Maria had picked up some type of colon infection, and they placed her on an extremely potent antibiotic for several weeks. At first she got better, but then her joints flared up again, at which point her family physician consulted me. His concern was whether she had an infected knee and whether surgery was required.

After examining her, I knew that her knee was not infected, but it was definitely swollen and irritated. When I compared notes with the infectious disease expert, it became clear to us that Maria was coming down with rheumatoid arthritis. She is doing fine now on the appropriate medicine.

At times, two or even three heads are far better than one! So if your doctor wants to get a second opinion, don't hesitate to do so. And if you and your wife are not happy with the way things are going, then get a second opinion. Or if you just want confirmation of the diagnosis and treatment, get a second opinion.

If you are in an HMO insurance plan, you may feel that you are locked in to seeing only the HMO doctor you have signed up with or been assigned. But what happens if you are not happy with that doctor, if things are not going right and you want a second opinion and the doctor won't refer you for that second opinion? You may think that you have to pay for it all out of your own pocket and have no recourse, but that is usually not true. Although most HMOs won't tell you, they have an appeal mechanism and a complaint department. If you call the insurance office and complain and are at all forceful or can explain your concern and the need for a second opinion, any good HMO will refer you to another physician for that second opinion. Believe me, I know these departments exist, so don't hesitate to avail yourself of what is rightfully yours. You will probably still need to be treated by a participating physician in the HMO, but at least you may be able to get another opinion.

I know this frustration. I diagnosed my best friend's son's knee condition in my family room and knew that he was going to require arthroscopic surgery. But in spite of the fact that I was willing to do the operation for nothing and the boy and his parents wanted me to do the surgery, they were in an HMO that precluded them from coming to me; even if I had waived my fee, they still would have had to pay the hospital charges out of their own pockets, which would have been prohibitive for them.

Welcome to the brave new world of health care!

When your wife is seriously ill, you gain a whole new understanding of what "one flesh" means. While your involvement and caring and love draw you and your wife together and deepen your relationship, they also help her get well or increase her chances of surviving.

Your wife truly needs you. If you follow these steps, she will do better, you will do better, your marriage will do better, and God will bless you and your marriage.

CHAPTER

9

Why Her?
Why Me?
Why Us?

Once you have both gotten over the shock of the diagnosis of your wife's illness or once you are in the midst of the stresses of dealing with it, the three most common questions you will probably ask yourself and God are: *Why us? Why me? Why her?* These are natural questions.

Down through the ages, prophets, theologians, philosophers, and individual men and women have always struggled with "Why do bad things happen? Why do we suffer?" Especially since the Bible says that God is going to bless us. But the Bible also describes how the wicked seem to prosper and the good always seem to suffer. The entire book of Job deals with such issues and questions.

One of the most normal and human responses to sickness or injury, especially when it is serious, is anger that this has happened to *us*—and anger *at God* that this has happened to us. Why did He do this to us?

Some people respond to these questions and reactions by saying, "It is sin! Sin caused this!"

I firmly believe that in certain cases sin can and does cause physical and emotional and mood symptoms. Unconfessed or unaddressed sinful behavior can lead to doubt and anger and depression. It can also cause headaches, stomach or bowel problems, back and joint pain, fatigue, and other physical symptoms that will stump physicians because they can find no "physical explanation" for the symptoms.

I do not believe, however, that all illness is punishment for sin. The Bible seems to indicate that it is rare for an illness to be punishment from God for sinful behavior.

Examples of such punishment can be found in both the Old and New Testaments. In 2 Kings 5, we read that Elisha's servant, Gehazi, was punished with leprosy for lying and stealing. Centuries later, during the days of the early church, Ananias and Sapphira were struck dead in front of Peter and the apostles when the couple lied to the Holy Spirit about the amount of money they had to give to the church (Acts 5).

Even King David, the man after God's own heart, bore such punishment:

Then David said to Nathan, "I have sinned against the Lord."

Nathan replied, "The Lord has taken away your sin. You are not going to die. But because by doing this you have made the enemies of the Lord show utter contempt, the son born to you will die."

After Nathan had gone home, the Lord struck the child that Uriah's wife had borne to David, and he became ill. . . . On the seventh day the child died. (2 Samuel 12:13–15, 18)

In each of these episodes illness and death are clearly a punishment for sinful behavior. But they are unique and specific instances, and each follows a certain pattern.

First of all, there is no connection between the behavior and the illness. Lying does not cause leprosy. Lying and cheating in matters of finance do not routinely lead to heart attacks, strokes, and death. Adultery and murder do not automatically lead to infant mortality. In each of these cases, the illness was not the logical consequence of behavior.

Second, in each instance, the sinner was told by a direct authority from God that his or her illness was a direct result of sinful behavior. The prophet Elisha told Gehazi, the apostle Peter told Ananias and Sapphira, and the prophet Nathan told King David, "Thus saith the Lord." So Gehazi, Ananias, Sapphira, and David did not have to ask, "Lord, why is this happening to me?" They knew. They had been told in no uncertain terms by men they knew were spokesmen of God.

It is tempting and, unfortunately, common for Christians to be judgmental in spite of what the Bible teaches about illness and punishment and the good suffering. Many still believe that if something bad happens it is because of something the person has done and that he or she "deserves" it as punishment. Yet Matthew 7:1 commands: "Do not judge, or you too will be judged."

It is not for any of us to judge why something happens to someone else. In the examples we used, look at who gave the notifications: Nathan the prophet, Elisha the prophet, and Peter the apostle. Obviously God had communicated these special messages to them. Unless people have that kind of authority, their words carry no weight. Remember, King David, Gehazi, and Ananias and Sapphira did not struggle with "Why is this happening to me?" They knew why!

Today, if an illness is punishment for sin, God, through the Holy Spirit, will convict the afflicted individual. It is not for us to judge and pronounce sentence—even when the person is someone we know as intimately as our spouse. While she may give you clues and a general sense of where she stands spiritually, ultimately only she knows what her relationship with God is.

In my experience, sin is an uncommon cause of illness. And if unrepented sin is at the heart of a mood disorder or other physical suffering, the afflicted person will already be under the conviction of the Holy Spirit—even if he or she denies it outwardly.

Let's move, then, to the most common causes of illness.

Number One: *Fifty percent of all illness in the United States is a direct result of lifestyle: the food we eat, the things we do, the life we lead.*

The heart disease, heart attacks, and strokes that are the major health concerns of our culture are the results of our high-fat and high-calorie diets, our high-stress lifestyles, and our lack of exercise.

Also, we do stupid things. When we do participate in sporting activities we often run into each other, bang into each other, and then are surprised when someone is hurt. Injuries in sports are predictable.

"That was the dumbest thing I ever did" is the line I hear frequently in my office when someone has been hurt working around the house—such as by cleaning leaves out of gutters and not propping the ladder correctly! I have yet to hear an adult say, "I was doing the right thing in the right place at the right time," when something like this happens. They always say, "That was the dumbest thing I ever did!" In other words, they got hurt while doing something they knew was putting them in jeopardy.

When we combine diet, lifestyle, the stress of our culture, the pollution of our environment, smoking, excessive alcohol consumption, and sexual promiscuity, is it any wonder people get sick? It is the logical consequence of our behavior.

Number Two: *Approximately one-third of all illness is genetic.* If your mother-in-law has crippling arthritis, there is a reasonable chance your wife will suffer some form of arthritis. Breast cancer clearly runs in families, as does colon cancer.

As the study of genetics progresses, we are learning that more and more diseases are inherited. I don't profess to understand the full impact of or meaning behind "sins of the father being visited upon second and third generations," but it is clear that some of us will pass on tendencies to certain diseases that we ourselves inherited from our parents.

So lifestyle, behavior, choices we make, and genetics account for over eighty percent of all disease and illness.

Number Three: *Finally, of course, there are instances when we just cannot explain "why."* Why does one person get sick as a result of lifestyle while another, doing or acting the very same way, does not?

This takes us back to the questions we raised at the beginning of the chapter. Throughout our lives all of us encounter unknowns, uncertainties, and what we may see as "unfairness."

Why, O Lord, do you stand far off?
Why do you hide yourself in times of trouble?

In his arrogance the wicked man hunts down the weak,
who are caught in the schemes he devises.
He boasts of the cravings of his heart;
he blesses the greedy and reviles the Lord.
In his pride the wicked does not seek him;
in all his thoughts there is no room for God.
His ways are always prosperous;
he is haughty and your laws are far from him;
he sneers at all his enemies. . . .

Arise, Lord! Lift up your hand, O God.
Do not forget the helpless.
Why does the wicked man revile God?
Why does he say to himself,
"He won't call me to account"?
But you, O God, do see trouble and grief;
you consider it to take it in hand.
The victim commits himself to you;
you are the helper of the fatherless.
—Psalm 10:1–5, 12–14

Here and elsewhere the psalmist struggled with these issues, as did many other writers of Scripture.

The Bible also provides ample evidence that God does use times of difficulty and physical suffering to strengthen our faith and our spirits. Suffering and hardship can draw us closer to God in a way nothing else can.

My son, do not despise the Lord's discipline and do not resent his rebuke, because the Lord disciplines those he loves, as a father the son he delights in. (Proverbs 3:11)

Blessed is the man whom God corrects; so do not despise the discipline of the Almighty. For he wounds, but he also binds up; he injures, but his hands also heal. From six calamities he will rescue you; in seven no harm will befall you. (Job 5:17–19)

No discipline seems pleasant at the time, but painful. Later on, however, it produces a harvest of righteousness and peace for those who have been trained by it. Therefore, strengthen your feeble arms and weak knees. "Make level paths for your feet," so that the lame may not be disabled, but rather healed. (Hebrews 12:11–13)

We need to be aware, however, that the promises in these verses do not mean that we will always be healed of illness. Just as there is the paradoxical promise of blessing and suffering so there is the apparent paradox of healing and those who continue to suffer and are not "healed." (We will talk about this in greater detail in chapter 16.)

God may use illness, afflictions, and injuries as discipline to draw us closer to Him. But this is not punishment; it is our Father training and disciplining His children. There may be behaviors we need to change or lessons we need to learn, and a time of illness can and should be a time to do this.

Few, if any, have ever suffered more than God's servant Job. Yet rather than resent his affliction as harsh discipline from the hand of the Lord, Job affirmed:

He knows the way that I take; when he has tested me, I will come forth as gold. (Job 23:10)

The book of Job contains many lessons for those who are suffering or hurting or for those who have loved ones who are suffering or hurting. One of the greatest lessons—which becomes evident after the questioning and accusations of Job's three "friends"—is that Job's illness was not punishment, it was not a direct result of his lifestyle, it was not caused by genetics, it wasn't for his own spiritual good, it wasn't to discipline him, and it wasn't to bring him back to God. It was a test. God let Satan test Job, and Job passed with flying colors.

I love the book of Job. Every time I read it and each time I hear it presented from the pulpit, I learn something new. Here are some of the lessons of Job that have helped me and may help you in the midst of your trials.

Lesson One: Job was a godly man. He was blessed abundantly in wealth and family and status and health.

Lesson Two: Job was a godly man. For this reason he suffered mightily. He lost family, lost all his children, lost all his wealth, lost all his status, and was grossly misjudged by his friends. The reason Job suffered was spiritual, but it was a spiritual tug-of-war between Satan and God. Job's suffering was all brought on by Satan. God permitted it, but He did not cause it.

Lesson Three: Job did not know why he was suffering. He did not know while he was suffering, he did not know when it was over, and he did not know even when he was blessed again. At no time was Job ever told why all of this happened to him.

Lesson Four: God chastised Job for even questioning and asking "why." When Job asked, "What have I done?" . . .

Then the Lord answered Job out of the storm.
He said:
"Who is this that darkens my counsel
with words without knowledge?
Brace yourself like a man;
I will question you,
and you shall answer me.

"Where were you when I laid the earth's foundation?
Tell me, if you understand.
Who marked off its dimensions? Surely you know!
Who stretched a measuring line across it?
On what were its footings set,
or who laid its cornerstone—
while the morning stars sang together
and all the angels shouted for joy?

"Who shut up the sea behind doors
when it burst forth from the womb,
when I made the clouds its garment
and wrapped it in thick darkness,
when I fixed limits for it
and set its doors and bars in place,
when I said, 'This far you may come and no farther . . . .'"
—Job 38:1–11

The Lord said to Job:
"Will the one who contends with the Almighty
    correct him?
Let him who accuses God answer him!"

Then Job answered the Lord:

"I am unworthy—how can I reply to you?
I put my hand over my mouth.
I spoke once, but I have no answer—
twice, but I will say no more."
—Job 40:1–5

It's almost as if God is saying, "Listen, you puny little worm, who do you think you are, questioning me?" Or like a slap upside the head, "Hey, wake up, boy, what do you think this is? Who do you think you are?"

Yet Job's response in questioning God is absolutely normal. It's what all of us do to a certain extent, some more than others. It is very natural when your wife is suffering for both of you to question why. It is natural to question God. Natural, but wrong.

Remember Job. None of the bad things that happened to him came from God. The dialogue between God and Job boils down to this: "Job, I am sovereign. I made you, I know what I am doing. You don't have the whole picture, and furthermore it is not for you to know."

Ultimately, when we are faced with trials and tribulations, we have to trust and believe in the sovereignty of God. God is in charge. He loves us, and He knows when we are suffering, and He hears our prayers.

God knows you and your wife are suffering, and He is in control.

CHAPTER

10

What about Our Social Life?

Megan teaches literature at a junior college and is a happily married mother of two. Her husband, Matt, is a successful stockbroker. One beautiful fall afternoon when the trees were bright with changing leaves, Matt suggested that, since the kids were busy with Saturday activities, the two of them should go for a drive around the lake and enjoy the scenery—something he knew Megan enjoyed.

Megan felt a migraine headache coming on, but she didn't want to disappoint Matt, so she didn't say anything. Eventually, however, she felt so miserable that she had to lay down in the back seat and slept through most of the color tour.

Matt felt the whole time was a wasted effort, and Megan felt bad because she had wrecked the trip for Matt.

Ken was an up-and-comer in his bank, so when the annual corporate party rolled around, he and his wife, Joan, planned to attend.

On the way to the party, however, Joan was hit full force with an attack of cramps and diarrhea. They couldn't even make it home. Ken had to find a gas station with a rest room, no mean trick in suburbia. Joan had suffered with this problem for years, usually triggered by stress and diet. Ken drove her home, but he was "too embarrassed" to go to the party late and alone, so he stayed home too.

Ken was aggravated and upset, which only added to the stress Joan already felt because of her untimely illness.

These are classic examples of how husbands and wives often fail to communicate and how illness can create misunderstanding and tension.

Part of the problem Ken had with Joan's illness was that he never really understood how much these social events stressed Joan. He knew she didn't like them, but since they never sat down and discussed her feelings and her reactions, he never really "got it" before this episode.

In the case of Megan and Matt, at the outset Megan should have been honest with Matt. She should have told him she was coming down with a migraine and needed to lie down in a dark bedroom and just let the headache run its course. She could have encouraged him to go out and enjoy the beauty of the afternoon himself.

Matt should then have been sensitive enough to say, "Hon, if you don't want to go, that's fine. We'll do it together when you're feeling better. Why don't you go lie down, and I'll head off to the course for a round of golf. The house will be quiet and you can get some rest."

Instead, both of them ended up doing something they didn't want to do and neither of them had a good time. Megan felt terrible because she had ruined Matt's afternoon. Matt felt bad because he had dragged Megan along and aggravated her headache—and, all things considered, he would rather have gone golfing anyway.

In the case of the second couple, Ken should have taken Joan home, made her comfortable, and then gone on to the company party if it was that important to him. Certainly this would have helped eliminate the hostility he felt, and it would have alleviated the stress and guilt Joan felt about ruining the evening.

Nothing gives you more opportunity for honest communication than situations like this.

Matt had never had a headache in his life, so he didn't understand how disabling and devastating migraine headaches are. Ken never had severe abdominal cramping of the type Joan suffered, not even when he had a bad case of the flu, so he didn't understand how disabling this was for Joan.

Part of caring for your wife is understanding the illnesses and symptoms she has. Whether or not stress precipitates them is immaterial; it doesn't change the degree of suffering or pain the person is experiencing. To truly care for someone you love, you need to be truly sympathetic to her suffering and condition. The only way to talk and openly about it.

A word of caution, though: The time for discussion is not when she is disabled with a headache or cramps or whatever the problem is. The time to talk is afterward; then ask her what you can do the next time she is ill or has these symptoms. Most often, people simply want to be left alone, and that is the nicest thing you can do—get her what she needs in the way of medication or comfort and then leave her in a quiet room in a quiet house.

But you won't know these things if you don't talk about them after an episode. If she tells you the best thing you can do is leave her alone, then trust her and do it. If she needs Pepto-Bismol, make sure there is a supply in the house.

BUSINESS AND SOCIAL OBLIGATIONS

I have been the president of the medical staff of three different hospitals; in that capacity I also served on the board of directors of these hospitals. This meant my wife and I were "expected" to attend a number of meetings and social functions every year. As time went on, however, it became increasingly difficult for us to get to these events. Often at the last minute—usually when we were getting dressed—Judy would either get sick or become panicked or anxious about going, and we would both stay home. Eventually, even though I expected this to happen, I would tell people we would attend; then we would end up arriving late or not at all. If we didn't go, I would later excuse our absence by exaggerating the severity of Judy's illness or symptoms.

It got to the point where I was missing meetings and functions that I truly needed to attend. At the last minute I was calling someone to cover my responsibilities, and occasionally I wouldn't even have the time to do that and could only hope they muddled through without me.

After several years of this, I realized that we needed to deal more openly and honestly with the situation. First of all, it had become apparent that Judy was simply not going to be able to go to most of these social functions. Second, I hated my own lying and deceit when I explained away our absence. And third, I was gaining a better understanding of the reasons behind Judy's anxiety and panic attacks.

Judy had started attending Adult Children of Alcoholics meetings and had begun reading widely on the subject. She encouraged me to read some of these books as well; I found them instructive and helpful in understanding her background and the effect it had had on her. Also, I found that the books were liberating for me, for they helped point out that my behavior was almost certainly destructive for both of us.

Judy hated the smell of beer because that was what her father drank. So any time she went where people were drinking beer, she hated it. She also hated the "socially liberating effects" of alcohol, the openness and "gaiety" people demonstrated when they were drinking. This reminded her of her young brother when he began drinking and the way his behavior would change dramatically; these memories brought back all the fear and stress she had felt then.

Judy and I had been married over fifteen years before I understood this. There was a short period of time, right after we were married, when both of us drank on social occasions. We stopped, but Judy was always afraid that I would start drinking as a result of attending these events. So she felt what I considered irrational fear of any social event where alcohol was going to be served, combined with her unease around those who were drinking and her gross distaste for the smell of beer. Unfortunately it took me fifteen years to realize how stressful these events were for her because of her childhood experiences around people who had been drinking.

Another destructive behavior was my need to make excuses for her and my "white lies" of deception.

Judy and I began to try to communicate more honestly, and I sat down and took a hard look at my meetings and social "obligations," attempting to assess their importance. As I did this, I began to identify four categories of business social events.

The first is *mandatory*—events or meetings that you and your wife, if at all possible, must attend. For example, if you are master of ceremonies or the speaker or are performing some other key function, then you had better show up. If you are applying for an appointment or a position and your potential employer wants to meet your wife, then you both need to be there. In the bigger scheme of things, there are really very few mandatory events.

The second category covers the *essential* meetings. These are good for your career and your standing with your company. Failure to show up might not cost you your job, but it might cost you a sale or a commission or an opportunity for advancement farther down the road. If all the spouses are attending such an event, it would be helpful if your wife were there with you.

The third category is what I call *encouraged* meetings— those you are encouraged to attend. It is hard to predict if not attending these will hurt your career or cost you sales or "clout," but it would certainly look better if you went. It does not matter at all if your wife comes to these meetings. In fact, when you analyze it all, it probably doesn't matter if you go either.

And the fourth category is *nonessential* meetings. It doesn't matter whether you go to these or not. Most social meetings or gatherings outside of work but associated with work probably fall into this category. It could be the Christmas dinner dance or the annual company picnic or the bowling league on Wednesday night. It might be nice for camaraderie, but whether you go or not really doesn't matter.

The older I get, however, the more apparent it is to me that even most of the encouraged and essential events are not all that important. If you don't go to the annual dinner or the office party, it is not going to affect your job. In fact, I think the career importance of these social engagements has been greatly exaggerated.

Once I had established these categories for myself, I had a way to assess and evaluate individual events as they arose. How important was it for me to attend? How vital was it for Judy to be there? Then the two of us would sit down and talk it over. Obviously our conversations aren't this cut-and-dried, but the following will give you the general idea.

If it was a mandatory meeting, I would explain its importance. "Judy, the other partners and I are having dinner with a new doctor we're thinking of bringing into the practice. His wife and the other spouses will be there, and I really would appreciate it if you could be there with me."

For the essential or encouraged meeting I would say, "Judy, I think it's a good idea for me to go to this meeting. It would be nice if you could come with me, but if you don't feel up to it, that's fine."

For the nonessential event I would simply tell her what it was and give her the option. "Judy, the office is going as a group to a Cubs' game, and I'm planning to go. I know you're not wild about baseball and you hate crowds, so if you don't want to come, that's fine." Or, "Judy, we have an opportunity to go to a fund-raiser and see *Phantom of the Opera.* If you want to go, I'll get the tickets. But I'm not interested in going by myself, so I need your commitment to go before I buy the tickets."

Even this kind of commitment was no guarantee that she would go. It took us years to come to grips with the fact that she would say she wanted to go to something and truly would want to go and still find that the stress before the event could precipitate an anxiety attack. Personally I still have to struggle with how it can be stressful for someone to do something they really want to do, but I know it is a fact. So if your wife is suffering this kind of problem, I can assure you that you are not alone and she is not doing it on purpose.

While our communication is better and the confrontations have been dramatically reduced, I don't want to imply that open communication will totally solve the problem. Sometimes it is just one of life's frustrations that you have to learn to deal with.

Another interesting thing I discovered was that when I would go to these meetings by myself I didn't mind telling the truth when someone asked where my wife was: "Judy hates coming to functions like this. She really gets claustrophobia in a crowd, so we decided I'd come by myself." Or, if she wasn't feeling well or was stressed, I'd be truthful about it, rather than exaggerating or making something up.

Just saying that my wife hates to come to meetings like this has engendered some incredible responses and admissions. Sometimes the wife of the couple I would be talking to would glare at her husband, as if to say, "See, this guy doesn't drag his wife out when she doesn't want to come!" I've never had a negative response. Often other men will say, "Here I thought my wife was the only one who hated coming to these things."

Also, I've frequently found that by going alone and being honest about it, I have much more open conversations with my coworkers and their spouses and, in fact, have sensed that they have more respect for both Judy and me and our relationship.

Probably my most important discovery, though, was how hard this whole thing had been on my wife and how destructive it had been to our relationship. I would get angry at her or disgusted with her or even wallow in self-pity, depending upon how I felt about the meeting or social engagement. Judy, in turn, would feel guilty or frustrated or depressed. My anger and hostility only aggravated the problems she was already struggling with and made her feel worse.

If you find yourself in this situation, I suggest that you and your wife sit down and honestly discuss any upcoming business and social engagements. When you do, I think you will find that there are very, very few events that are mandatory for your wife to attend. And you probably will be pleasantly surprised if you go by yourself and are honest about why your wife isn't there—as I was.

But, above all, it is unfair and potentially destructive for you to continually pressure your wife to attend such events or meetings. If you tell her it is essential that she be there and then she discovers that it is not, or that half the other spouses aren't there, or that you pressured her because you were afraid you would be embarrassed, this not only calls your honesty into question, but can be harmful for your future communication and your relationship.

Be honest about your own feelings and wishes, and allow your wife to be honest about hers.

Work-related social functions are not the only problem situations. Some of us may not even have to deal with those. But all of us have social functions related to church or family gatherings. In some ways, these can be even more stressful than a social event with "total strangers." And the principles we have talked about apply whether it is a family reunion, a Sunday school party, or church picnic, and whether it is a migraine headache, abdominal cramping, cancer, or arthritis that is hindering your wife's ability to attend and enjoy the event. You need to talk openly and honestly about how both of you feel about attending the event and how important it is to you. You also need to be brutally honest about your motives for going or not wanting to go.

Several times a year one of my wife's dear friends invites us over for dinner. I will gear myself up for these events, but I hate going, because for some reason my wife's friend's husband really distrusts doctors and he invariably ends up talking about how doctors have mistreated members of his family, or some similar topic. Since Judy knows I don't like going to these dinners, she only accepts a minimum amount of the invitations and gets together with her friend at other times instead.

If you are a deacon or an elder in your church, you may feel a special pressure to have your wife come to certain church functions that she doesn't feel comfortable going to or doesn't want to go to. While there are several New Testament verses that prescribe an acceptable home life for deacons and elders, none of these prescriptions apply to social events. So even if you hold such a position in your church, don't pressure your wife to attend something she doesn't want to attend. And again, examine your motives. Is your real reason for wanting her there to make you look good? Whatever the motive, admit it and deal with it appropriately.

All of us face these issues at some point in our married lives. My hope and prayer for you is that you and your wife will be communicating well enough and honestly enough so that social activities, whether they are work related or church related or pure pleasure, will be enjoyable times for both of you. You both need to be free to go or go alone or not go, but the only way that is going to happen is for you to have a trusting, loving, honest relationship with each other. That is the best way you can care for your wife.

MAINTAINING A BALANCE

When your wife suffers a temporary illness, it is often natural and appropriate to cancel activities you might be planning as a couple or as a family, or even something you might be doing on your own, so that you can be available to her. Clearly there are times when your wife is suffering that you should stay with her. To do otherwise demonstrates a gross lack of caring and compassion. But if your wife has a chronic or recurring illness, then you cannot focus exclusively on her illness and cancel all of your social activities. In fact, it is unhealthy for you, for her, and for your children (we'll talk more about your children in later chapters).

For a long time, I did exactly that myself. If Judy wasn't feeling well, I canceled any engagements we had planned. My thinking and feeling at the time was that if I couldn't go with Judy and enjoy it with her, then I wouldn't go at all. I wanted her to experience all the pleasurable things I did at these events, and deep down I wanted her to like doing these things as much as I did. I had accepted the "romantic notion" that we should do everything together as a couple.

During courtship and early marriage a man and woman want to do everything together—that's natural. But as a relationship matures, both men and women need their own "space"; they need to have some time to pursue and enjoy their own interests, activities, or hobbies. If you do not accept this fact and act on it, you are going to have real problems if your wife is ill for any length of time. You will have to cancel everything and essentially not do anything. This can be very destructive for both of you because . . .

— you are going to miss out on many things in life;

— your own mental and physical health will suffer as you are dragged down by lack of any social activities or exercise;

— your wife will bear the added burden of knowing that she is keeping you from doing things you enjoy and need.

I can tell you from personal experience that before long, as you miss out on more and more things, you will start to resent your wife's illness. Then you will feel guilty about having those feelings about someone you love who is sick and can't help it. You will begin to feel bad because you are mad at her. Then you will feel even more guilty because you will consider your anger childish. It's a vicious cycle.

The best way to avoid this is for the two of you to sit down and communicate honestly about what is happening and how you are both feeling. You need to categorize your activities and interests as to level of importance, desirability, and need. For example, exercise rates high in all three.

When Judy was really depressed, she didn't want me to leave her. She would be anxious and afraid—afraid, for example, that if I went out jogging I would have a heart attack and drop dead or get lost or get mugged. Most of these fears were irrational, but nonetheless real. So I started saying, "I am going to be gone for exactly thirty-five minutes (or whatever)" and I would make sure that I was back exactly when I said I would be.

This did alleviate her fears, but I found that to be effective, my timing had to be precise. In other words, if I said I was going to be gone for forty minutes, I had to return in forty minutes. The worst thing I could do was say I was only going to be gone for about half an hour and then be gone for an hour. I had to treat it like an important appointment, rather than just generalize the way I tend to do when I'm going for a run or off to the hardware store. (I know one woman who says that letting her husband go to the hardware store is like sending him into the Twilight Zone.)

If the activity is something like a sporting event, you need to deal with it equally forthrightly. For example, "Hon, I really want to go to the Bulls game next month." If she isn't interested, go by yourself or with your kids or friends. If she says she wants to go, get two tickets. Then if she opts out when the day arrives, take a friend or one of your children.

There will be times, of course, when the activity is something you absolutely do not want to do without her; it is something she really likes to do and without her it would not be enjoyable for you. In our case that could be something like a Peter, Paul, and Mary concert. In this situation, if you have the tickets and your wife's illness prevents her from going that night, you don't have to feel guilty about giving the tickets to someone else and staying home yourself.

The third category is a mixture of the two, that middle ground where the activity is something you would like to do yourself but would enjoy much more if you could do it with your wife. In this instance, you might want to agree ahead of time on a contingency plan if she is sick that night. It might go something like this: "Okay, hon, I am going to get two tickets for *Phantom of the Opera*. If you are not up to going that night, I'll either take one of the kids or let two of the kids go together" (or let your child take a friend, or whatever the logical plan might be, depending on how much you yourself want to see the show).

When your spouse has a chronic or recurring illness it is easy to get so caught up in the illness and its demands that you (and sometimes the rest of the family) become almost a social recluse. That is not healthy for you—or for your wife and your children. You certainly should not always be running off by yourself or neglecting your wife, but you also should not put pressure on her so that she either goes and feels wretched or stays home and feels guilty.

On the surface it sounds laudable to deny yourself these pleasures because your wife can't enjoy them with you; unfortunately this can begin to smack of martyrdom. You may even be relishing your martyrdom because you win sympathy for yourself—"what a fine fellow he is," or, "oh, you poor guy, look what you are going through."

One of the hardest things to do when you are caring for someone who is sick for a long period of time is to acknowledge your own needs and take care of yourself. In that situation you tend to ignore your own feelings and needs; frequently you'll forego your exercise routine or recreation and stop doing anything that is fun and nonessential. This is normal and natural in an acute crisis, but in an ongoing situation it is unhealthy for both of you.

When your wife suffers a lengthy illness it is also natural for friends and relatives to reassure you and be positive and tell you how caring you are and how tough this must be on you. It is also natural to take some pleasure in the fact that someone recognizes your care and devotion. The problem is that this can be seductive, and to combat this you may subconsciously continue to deny yourself, thinking that this will keep you from becoming proud of your struggle and proud of your behavior. That is a trap you want to avoid. To care for her you have to take care of yourself.

Be honest. Communicate with your wife; validate her feelings and yours. Be truthful about what you *want* to do, what you *have* to do, and what you *don't want* to do. Find out what she *wants* to do, what she *can* do, and how she *feels about* it. Then agree on a plan. Also, be truthful with your friends and associates. This is the healthiest approach. Through it, you will grow as an individual, and your relationship with your wife will become even stronger.

TRAVEL

Travel means different things to different people. To some it is adventure and excitement, to some it is drudgery and work, to some it is nausea from motion sickness, and to some it is terror from fear of flying or claustrophobia. (My mother-in-law survived the first commercial airline accident in this country and lost most of her family in that accident, so I don't think fear of flying is *totally* irrational.) To most of us, though, *business* travel means separation and isolation.

Business travel is an unavoidable fact of life for many men. Most of the time it is not pleasure; it is hard work. Salesmen, for example, must travel to do their job. Travel is a part of the job for many people in our mobile society, the most famous, of course, being professional athletes.

For me, business travel usually comes in the form of continuing medical education (CME hours are required by many states to maintain a medical license to practice) or annual medical society meetings (if you do not attend, you lose your membership). I don't have to attend every meeting, but I do have to attend enough to accumulate a certain number of hours each year.

Judy and I were married several years before I had to do any serious traveling. The annual orthopedic convention was in Chicago every other year; that required only a train ride or a short drive and I was not gone in the evenings. It was no different than a day at work. My travel really started after we had been married six or seven years and had several small children. When that happened, things changed.

Usually a day or two before I had to leave, Judy would begin questioning me—"Why do you have to go to the meeting? How important is it?"— and then pleading, "Do you really need to go?" She would become increasingly stressed, agitated, and even depressed. The longer we were married, the more predictable this scenario became, until I started to cancel trips simply because Judy seemed so stressed by my leaving, or because I was afraid that she would become so depressed when I was gone that she would require hospitalization. As soon as I canceled the trip, however, she would be fine.

Finally, of course, I would reach a point where I absolutely had to go in order to maintain my membership or obtain enough CMEs. Judy would still be very stressed and I would be very worried, but I would have no choice. So I'd take a deep breath, give her a hug, and leave, fearing the worst. Interestingly enough, once I got to the meeting and called home, Judy would be fine.

After Judy had been in therapy for a while and we had talked about it at length and read many books on the subject, it became apparent that this anxiety dated back to her childhood and was rooted in fear of separation. She was afraid that I would not return and she would be left alone. The first time she told me this, I had trouble even believing it! From my perspective it was totally irrational. But no matter how it sounded to me, it didn't change the way Judy felt.

Now we both face up to the stress Judy experiences when I leave. Where before I was angry and disgusted by her reactions, although I tried to hide it, now we talk it through and I understand my wife better.

Symptoms and illnesses that occur when the need to travel arises are often the result of subconscious reactions to earlier stresses, and the older we get, the worse these symptoms usually become. John Madden, the famous football coach and announcer, used to fly with his team, but the older he got, the harder it was for him to fly—and now he doesn't fly at all. He has his own bus and arranges his schedule to allow for travel time.

My wife suffers from a chronic sinus problem, and the rapid decompression in airplanes frequently gives her disabling headaches; she also can get very claustrophobic and stressed being closed in an airplane. She will say that she really wants to make an upcoming trip, but the stress of being in the plane and the fear of the possible headaches force her to cancel out at the last minute. It has taken us years to understand and come to grips with this. We have accepted the fact that it is never going to go away completely, and we are working on it together.

Let me also tell you that while you may get upset or angry if this happens to you, deep inside your wife is even more upset or angry with herself because of the impact her symptoms are having on both of you.

Thus, I would recommend that you deal with travel, particularly business travel, the same way you do social engagements and business events. The difference here, of course, is that clearly most business travel is mandatory or essential. There are times, however, when business meetings are held in attractive locations or resorts that spouses would enjoy. So when it comes to travel, apply a decision-making process similar to the ones we discussed above.

I guess by now you realize that we are dealing with one overriding principle here: If you really want to care for your wife, you must learn to communicate with her. You have to come to the point in your relationship where you are absolutely honest with each other. You both need to be free enough and mature enough to go to business or social events alone and to trust each other when one of you says, "It doesn't matter. I don't mind going alone." Or, "It doesn't matter. Go and have a good time." And you need to care enough for each other that these lines are not delivered or intended as an underlying sarcasm of "Poor me. I'll go alone." Or, "Poor me. I'll stay home alone."

Communicating honestly is a big step toward truly caring for your wife.

"Dr. Dominguez, you saved my life," said Maggie. "I feel like a new woman. That was the best advice I ever got."

Two weeks earlier, Maggie, a nurse-anesthetist I worked with, had been complaining while we were in surgery that her teenage stepdaughters were driving her crazy with their demands on her time. Maggie was working full-time and was also in a new marriage.

I about jumped over the ether screen as I said, "Maggie! My ten-year-old son does his own laundry. Stop doing their laundry."

"I can't do that," Maggie said. "It will be a disaster Saturday night when they are all set to go out and have 'nothing to wear.'"

Chapter 11

"Maggie," I said, "sit the girls down and spell out the rule of the house—do your own laundry. Then teach them how to do it. Show them how to use the washer and dryer. Explain about colors and whites and delicate cycles. If they are smart enough to attend high school, they are smart enough to do their own laundry! Then tell them that from now on they are responsible for their own laundry—and follow through on it. I guarantee you, Maggie, after the first time some social event comes up and they have nothing to wear, it will never happen again."

That's exactly what happened. And Maggie's life was changed simply because her teenagers started doing laundry.

My wife, Judy, is a terrific mother. In dedicating my first book to her, I paid tribute to this fact by saying that "her boys will never have red underwear." It was interesting to me that a lot of people didn't understand that comment. Well, any guy who has ever lived in a men's college dorm or bached it understands what red underwear is all about. It's what happens when you've never been taught how to do laundry and you throw all your clothes in the washing machine at the same time. Red underwear.

Judy and I have nine children, and the only way you can survive with nine children is to have a routine. All of our children have been required to make their own beds and clean up their rooms. We have some messy daughters and some neat sons, and we have some messy sons and some neat daughters. But they all make their own beds and clean their own rooms—even though individual quality and haste may vary.

From age eight on, they make their own lunches. We teach them how and make sure the ingredients are in the fridge or the cupboard, but putting the lunch together is their responsibility. And when they are ten or eleven years old, they're taught to do their own laundry. When they are a bit older, they also do their own ironing.

THE IMPORTANCE OF ROUTINE

Children love routine. They need routine. So do parents. Illness plays havoc with routine. If your children have already been taught the "survival skills" mentioned above, it will help immeasurably. That is one less stress you and your wife have to worry about if she becomes ill. If your children are small, of course, the situation is different.

When my wife was hospitalized with encephalitis for almost three weeks, we truly understood the value of a large family. I had a busy medical practice and four little kids at home. My mother moved in with us, and the children's routine never changed. Also, during those weeks the church provided meals for us every day. In fact, we had more food than we knew what to do with.

If your wife becomes seriously ill and is unable to function for a time, my hope and prayer is that you either have a large extended family or belong to a church that will function as an extended family. The small group movement in many churches is an active part of such ministry. When there is illness in one of their church families, the group pitches in to help with everything from meals to car pooling and baby-sitting. Managing such daily routines can be particularly stressful while you are trying to maintain your own work schedule—and even more so if your job requires travel.

If none of these options are available, you will have to hire someone to move in with you or farm your children out to friends or relatives—a last resort in my book. Children experience enough stress when Mom is sick, without the added stress of disrupting their routine and leaving their home and Dad.

Chapter 11

Some jobs or professions are flexible enough or some employers understanding enough that you can juggle your hours in order to run errands or pick up the children from day care or school, but my experience says that is the exception rather than the rule.

"No man is an island" is never more true than when your wife is sick and you have children. You can't do it alone; you need help. So don't be afraid to ask for it and look for it and accept it when it is offered to you.

As far as meals go, if it is a long-term or recurring illness, you will need to make some permanent adjustments. Church groups burn out after a while, and you can't expect them to provide your meals for an extended period of time.

If you know how to cook, you'll definitely have an advantage (another argument for teaching your children some self-sufficiency, which may well pay off in their own later years). But today's supermarkets and delis offer everything from lasagna to baked chicken. And in a pinch you can always fall back on the four basic food groups: Wendy's, McDonald's, Pizza Hut, and Burger King!

Don't allow the latter to become the daily menu, however. Kids may survive indefinitely on junk food, but they shouldn't. Do your best to give them a healthy, balanced diet.

Which brings us to another point: Just because Mom is sick doesn't mean the kids can get away with murder!

Discipline tends to be neglected or ignored in times of crisis. While you need to be understanding and appreciate that your children are upset and feel the stress of the situation just as you do, you should not allow this to become an excuse for bad behavior. Bend a little, as circumstances dictate, while still maintaining discipline. If you don't, that in itself will cause your children additional stress. All of which cycles back to routine. Children need routine; they take solace in routine. And routine itself makes discipline easier, because your children already know what is required of them.

Having said this, I would also caution you to be careful about any punishments you mete out when you are stressed yourself. At times like that, be slower to react, back off, take some deep breaths. Don't take your own stress out on your children. That is unfair, harmful, and could be incredibly destructive. Don't slack up on your discipline; but don't get stricter either.

Just remember, when Mom is ill . . .
— your children are just as stressed as you are;
— your children need your understanding;
— your children need you to listen to them;
— your children need you to give them each time;
— your children need you to answer their questions.

THE IMPORTANCE OF PRAYER

If you don't already do this, begin praying each night with each child before he or she goes to sleep.

This nightly routine does two things: first, it teaches your children the value of a regular prayer and devotional life; second, as you listen to what your children verbalize in their prayers, you begin to have a better understanding of their concerns. This gives you insight into what they are thinking and reveals areas where they need reassurance. Be prepared for some surprises, however, for your child's concern may be entirely different from anything you ever imagined.

On the night before Judy was to go into the hospital for routine surgery, I was praying with my girls, and both of them prayed, "Dear Lord, please don't let Mommy die or have cancer." Neither of these thoughts had ever occurred to me because, of course, I knew the surgery was so routine that cancer was never an issue, nor was it any type of life-threatening procedure. The girls, of course, were looking at it from their own perspective and experience. Their beloved Uncle Jim had died the year before of cancer and another uncle had just been in for a biopsy that turned out to be cancer. So to my girls, going to the hospital and having surgery meant cancer.

During these prayer times, encourage your children to pray for Mom and for her healing. Our children need to know that God is concerned with our well-being, our health, our fears, and our concerns. As time passes, you will be able to discuss with your children the results of these prayers and the answers God has given.

If Mom gets better, the children need to be reminded that God did hear their prayers and that her recovery is a positive answer. If Mom isn't getting better, this needs to be discussed also. This is always tougher, of course.

My children constantly hear me quoting, "Life ain't fair," because fairness is an important issue for kids. This shouldn't be surprising. Don't we adults still struggle with why good people suffer and get sick?

Our children need to know that bad things happen to good people and that many times we don't know why. They need to know that while God does hear our prayers, He doesn't always answer the way we want Him to.

You must point out to them that even if they haven't gotten the answer they wanted or the answer hasn't been given yet, God still hears them and loves them. He doesn't always give us the answer we want, and His timetable is usually different than our timetable. In today's instant-gratification culture, it is especially important that our children learn that praying to God is not like going to McDonald's or Burger King: we do not get instantaneous answers on demand, and we cannot always "have it our way." Patience and waiting on Him is something we have to learn.

Praying with your children will help keep your lines of communication open with them and with God. But there is other communication regarding your children that is also important.

THE IMPORTANCE OF COMMUNICATION

If you are going to get the help you need in caring for your children when your wife is ill, you will have to communicate the situation to your family, friends, and church. I am constantly amazed at how little most of us tell our friends and relatives about what is really going on in our lives. I know you may find it difficult to ask for help, but you need to do it—if only for the sake of your children. Family and friends will not know how they can help if they don't even know there is a problem.

You also absolutely must communicate with your children's teachers. While your children may behave normally at home, the stress of their mother's illness will sometimes show up in their classwork or their behavior in school. If the teachers are aware of the situation at home, they can watch for any effect it may have on your child's schoolwork. Most teachers will also be more understanding and helpful regarding your child's needs if they understand that there is illness in the home.

If your kids are in elementary school, talk to their teachers directly. If your kids are high school age, it will probably be easier to go through the school counselor and let him or her communicate the information to the appropriate teachers.

If your child has a Christian schoolteacher or attends a Christian school, this can be an added advantage; the school and the teachers may well begin to pray for your family and your child.

WHAT IF MOM IS IN THE HOSPITAL?

Nowadays it is unusual for anyone to stay in the hospital for any length of time. If your wife's hospital stay is only for twenty-four to forty-eight hours, then it may not be necessary or even worth the effort to take the children to see her. But if she is going to be hospitalized for any length of time, your children should visit her in the hospital.

One exception to this would be if her condition is so severe or grave that you feel it would be too traumatic for your children, especially if she is unconscious or hooked up to a respirator; another exception is if your wife is on a psychiatric ward or in a psychiatric hospital. In that case, the children may not be permitted to visit anyway, especially if she is on a "locked ward."

Whenever possible, however, I strongly encourage children to visit, no matter how bad their mother looks or feels, because children need to *know*—to see—that Mom is alive. The longer she is gone, the more apprehensive and anxious they become and the more difficult it is to reassure them. When they can't *see* her, children imagine the worst. I can't emphasize enough how important it is for children to see their mother and know that she is alive and getting better.

Most hospitals permit children of any age to visit. Also, if her condition allows it, you may be able to take your wife to the lounge or cafeteria where the children can visit her. Even if she is on a psychiatric ward, visitation can be arranged. Once her doctor agrees that she is up to seeing the children, he can give her a pass to visit them in the cafeteria or lounge.

Most good nurses are very understanding about children visiting Mom, even if it is against "the rules." In cases of extended illness, the hospital staff is usually very under-standing.

The other side of the coin, of course, is that some children are afraid to go to a hospital and afraid of seeing Mom when she is ill. If that is the case, don't force them to go; respect their fears and concerns. You should, however, try to determine why they are afraid so you can help them deal with that fear. Young children may not be able to verbalize their fear, but as you draw them out, you have another opportunity to communicate honestly with them.

When your children do visit their mother, set a time limit for the visit. I usually recommend fifteen minutes. That allows enough time to let them see Mom, give her a hug, and talk to her. Anything longer than that and they are going to start getting antsy, especially young children. And if your wife is sick enough to be in the hospital, anything longer than fifteen minutes is going to be very tiring for her. Certainly anything more than thirty minutes is going to be too exhausting and stressful.

If at all possible, make sure that your children get to hold Mom's hand and hug and kiss her during the visit. At times this is not possible, especially the hugging and kissing, but those times are rare—for example, if she is suffering from something contagious. In that case, though, you would be taking the needed precautions anyway. Actually, physical contact is usually more of a problem if the kids are sick and have something contagious, like strep throat or a cold or the flu, in which case it would be wise not to bring them to the hospital at all—for everyone's sake.

When Mom is in the hospital, your children may have trouble sleeping and may want to sleep with you. This is a normal response. There is nothing wrong with letting them occasionally crawl into bed with you for a few minutes or jump in bed with you in the morning when you are all waking up; this can be fun and offers moments of warm and comforting bonding. They may even sleep in the same room with you, either camping out on the floor or on a couch. (Children can easily sleep on the floor with a blanket—their young bones and muscles won't ache in the morning!) However, you should not let your school-age children sleep with you the whole night.

There is potential for sexual overtone and subtle types of abuse if you sleep with your child alone. I am not a child psychologist, so we are not going to get into a long discussion on this subject. Suffice it to say that it is probably not a good idea for school-age children to sleep with you when your wife isn't there. During an extremely stressful time preschoolers may require your nearness for security, but that, too, is something you need to end as soon as possible.

WHAT DO I TELL THE KIDS WHEN MOM IS SICK?

First and foremost, tell them the truth. If you lie to them or try to deceive them, they will lose their trust in you. Also, you will be teaching them, by your behavior, that it is all right to lie.

If Mom can't go ice skating with you because she is sick, tell the kids that. If they want more details, tailor your answer to what is appropriate for their age and the situation.

Remember, their experience is much more limited than yours, and they will assume things based on their experiences thus far in life.

If Uncle Jim went to the hospital because he "wasn't feeling well" and two weeks later Uncle Jim was dead, and then you say, "Mom is going to the hospital because she doesn't feel well," your child may assume that two weeks later Mom will die.

Answer your children's questions at their level of understanding. Don't embellish too much or provide them with more information than they need or can comprehend.

If your wife is going to the hospital for minor surgery, your four-year-old may ask, "Is Mommy going to die?" Of course the appropriate answer is, "Mommy is going to be fine and she'll be home soon."

If your wife is depressed and your child asks, "What's wrong with Mom?" don't be afraid to say, "Mom is depressed today," or "Mom is feeling down right now." Often with younger children this is all you have to say. You answer the question, and bang! they run off to play.

With older children, however, resist any temptation to go into lengthy discussions. Give them age-appropriate explanations, but do not treat your child as a surrogate spouse and, in a sense, cry on his or her shoulder. This can be particularly tempting when your wife's illness falls into the mood disorder category. I know parents who have done this, and it is a form of emotional child abuse. It is not healthy for you, it is not healthy for your relationship with your wife, and it is certainly not healthy for your child.

It is incredibly important to keep the lines of communication open, so always answer your children's questions honestly and at an age-appropriate level. Children want and need to be reassured that everything is going to be okay. Whenever it is appropriate and the truth, reassure them that, while Mom is sick right now, she will get better and everything will be all right.

If your wife is terminally ill or has a chronic incurable condition, then you need to address that honestly and openly in an age-appropriate way. Don't fall into the trap of trying to reassure children falsely if Mom has something incurable. If you don't tell them the truth regarding this, they may never trust you again.

If your wife has an addiction, that creates all kinds of unique problems. Psychologists frequently use the term "shame-based" to describe these types of problems because the non-addicted spouse is ashamed of the alcoholic or addicted spouse, and the children learn to be ashamed as well.

In these situations, children learn four house rules:

1. Don't feel. (Alcoholics frequently lose their self-control and in temper or rage take it out on their children. The discipline they mete out can be brutal. Because the non-alcoholic parent is frequently in denial or intent on his or her own survival issues, the child has no parent to turn to for sympathy or understanding, so the early lesson is "Don't feel any emotion.")

2. Don't talk. ("Don't air our dirty laundry in public.")

3. Don't trust. (Children raised in these kinds of house-holds are frequently abused. Because they can't trust their parents, they don't trust any adults.)

4. Don't need. (The nonalcoholic parent has a tendency to be so concerned with survival issues and dealing with the alcoholic partner that the children's needs, even many of their basic physical needs, are ignored.)

As tough or as tragic as your situation may be with an addicted spouse, don't compound the damage by passing on these distortions to your children. If your spouse is alcoholic or addicted, you are going to need help in caring for her, but don't forget your children. They do have feelings and you must talk honestly with them. You must be the person and the parent they can trust. Don't ignore their emotional, physical, spiritual, and other needs. Don't compound the problem by not paying attention to your children.

If Mom is drunk, the worst thing you can say is, "She's fine. Don't worry about it." She is not fine; she is drunk. And when the kids ask what is wrong, they need to be told that Mom has been drinking too much and is drunk. The worst thing you can do is pretend that this is normal and all right.

Sadly, there is alcoholism in Christian families. Some might want to deny that, but it's a fact. I have never attended a church where there was not at least one regular attender or member who was married to an alcoholic. So if your spouse is an alcoholic or addicted, you can rest assured that you are not the only Christian going through such trials. But don't try and cover up the problem and deny that it exists. If you do that, you are falling into the same trap that alcoholic families have always fallen into and creating terrible problems for your own children. On top of that, it is an unchristian thing to do; it is lying.

Children raised in alcoholic families describe this as "the rhinoceros in the living room." Something is obviously, desperately wrong, but everybody pretends nothing is wrong. There is a rhinoceros in the living room, but everybody pretends it is not there. Whatever you do, don't foster the kind of shame-based communication that pretends there is no problem. This is very destructive for your children. (If you need any further proof, just look at the number of groups such as Adult Children of Alcoholics—adults who are just now coming to grips with the damage they have suffered from being raised in alcoholic families.)

Children need to be taught that emotions are fine. If Mom is sick and you are unhappy about it, your children need to know that. If Mom is drunk and you are unhappy about it, they need to know that.

Children need to be able to talk openly and honestly with you about family problems. And they need you to be honest with them. To say everything is all right when it obviously isn't is not open, honest communication.

And what should your children tell their friends? Second verse, same as first: "the truth"—within the bounds of family privacy of course. Sit down with your children and give them the ground rules on what truthful things they can say about Mom, rather than leave it up to them to decide. Tell them that family privacy is important and that their friends don't need to know the full details of Mom's illness. Most children will honor these conditions if you openly discuss them.

Children need to learn to trust—and that begins at home with their parents. They need to know that you are going to listen to them, that you are going to communicate with them honestly, and that they can trust you with their concerns.

Children do have needs, and their needs have to be met. That is one reason their routine should be disrupted as little as possible. Our children need our communication, they need our love, they need us.

Here are ten commandments for dealing with your children:

1. *Always tell the truth.*

2. *Don't insist nothing is wrong if one parent is sick or behaving strangely.*

3. *Don't assume your children are oblivious to emotional undercurrents.*

4. *Always keep the lines of communication open.*

5. *Be alert to what children may overhear.*

"Children are the world's best tape recorders and the world's worst interpreters."

6. *Watch what you blurt out in anger or when you are stressed.*

Children take things literally.

7. *If you and your wife have had an argument or a fight and your children have witnessed or overheard it, admit that the two of you have had a difference of opinion.*

Arguments or fights occur in every marriage. To deny something the children have heard is deceitful, wrong, and harmful. You don't need to go into any great explanation; just admit that sometimes you and Mom disagree but you are going to work it out.

8. *Constantly reassure them.*

Remember, children frequently will blame themselves for family problems or illnesses. To reassure them, it is important to keep the lines of communication open.

9. *If your wife is irritable or cranky or unreasonable because of PMS or menopause or some other hormonal problem, explain that to the children in an age-appropriate way.*

Simply acknowledge the problem and get the kids out of the way for a few hours. (One woman author says that she used to tell her children that these outbursts were the results of her menopausal hormonal changes and that she was acting like "Menomama"; they would laugh about it together, and it would help relieve the tension.)

10. *Tell your children often and daily that you love them and that God loves them. Hug and kiss them every day.*

To summarize: When Mom is sick . . .

Tell your children the truth, even if you don't know how serious the outcome is going to be, or even if things aren't going well.

Don't disrupt your children's lives any more than necessary. Try to keep their schedules unchanged and their routine the same. Children find great security in routine.

Don't stop having fun with your children.

Don't change "the rules of the house." Chores and homework have to be done, bedtime must be adhered to, and discipline should not be ignored.

THE PARENT TRAP

In the movie *Mrs. Doubtfire*, Robin Williams plays a father who is devoted to his children; he plays with his kids all the time and does all kinds of wild and crazy things that delight them. He is also totally irresponsible. His wife, played by Sally Field, is not only the primary breadwinner, but has been forced to come on as the heavy to compensate for her husband's lack of discipline and general lack of responsibility. In law enforcement this is called good cop-bad cop, where to get results one person comes on heavy and the other offers a sympathetic buffer. It may work there, but it doesn't work in the home.

When your wife is sick, however, this is a trap you can fall into. If you cancel all fun events, your children begin to see their mother as the person who is keeping them from going places and doing things. Or, they might begin to see Dad as the only parent they can have fun with.

If your wife is suffering a temporary illness, this probably won't be an issue, and putting certain activities on hold will be the appropriate way to go. But if your wife is suffering a chronic or recurring illness, you can't stop the world.

Personally, there were times in the past when Judy was ill that I would cancel things we were going to do with the children or not schedule activities because I wanted us all to be together as a family. I was afraid I would do all the fun things with the kids and Judy wouldn't get to do anything with them. Consequently none of us did anything!

If you fall into this trap, your children will suffer. It is vital that you, as much as possible, minimize the effect of your wife's illness on your family lifestyle. A good basic principle is do what you can as a family and do it together; when that is not possible, make other arrangements rather than disappoint the children and deny them opportunities they should have. (You can adapt some of the same decision-making procedures and communication opportunities that were suggested in chapter 10.)

If the activity is something you want to do with the kids or that you and the kids want to do together, then do it. If you don't, your wife will feel bad or guilty. Also, you may subconsciously resent the fact that she prevented you from doing something with the kids that you wanted to do or that they wanted to do.

Part of the problem, too, is that kids are terrific at reading body language. So even if you don't tell them you canceled the trip to the zoo because of their mother's illness, they will know. Then you are back into the good cop-bad cop situation, which is not healthy for any of you. And the worst thing you can do is lie to your children about the reason you are canceling. Again, they will find out, and you will have betrayed their trust and set a terrible example.

Make every effort to do things as a family, but recognize that there are times when you simply can't do that.

Also, make time to do one-on-one things with each of your children. Kids cherish the time they have you alone. The more children you have, the more important this becomes.

Psychologists and educators make a big deal about "quality time" spent with children. My experience and strong conviction is that it is an overused term and concept. I believe you have to spend "quantities of time" with your children—and out of that quantity come quality moments. Quality is not something you can schedule; it is something that happens when you give it the opportunity to happen. And you do that by spending quantities of time with children.

When my wife is unable to travel, I often take one of our older children with me. This is something the kids and I look forward to, and traveling together has provided some real quality moments.

Hook, the latest movie version of the story of Peter Pan, begins with a boy's championship Little League baseball game. His father (a grown-up Peter Pan), a hard-charging, financially successful businessman, promises the son that he will make the game. The little boy is constantly looking over his shoulder for his father, but his father never gets there. While he is looking for his father, the boy messes up and costs the team the championship.

The boy's failure is blamed on the father's failure to show up for the son's performance, and the rest of the movie is based upon the little boy's rejection of his father because of this offense.

In today's culture one of the "standards" is that you must not miss any of your children's games or performances or competitions. Being a parent of nine, I often have several children "performing" at different places at the same time. Early on, our children learned that Dad and Mom can't be at more than one place at the same time, so they don't expect us to be at every performance or competition.

As a parent and a physician whose specialty is sports medicine, I have good reason to reject this popular suburban standard that you have to attend all of your children's games and performances. And I categorically reject the thesis in the movie *Hook*—that our children's failures are somehow our fault. In fact, true achievers are those who are internally motivated to be successful, rather than those who only perform when their parents are in the audience.

To be truly great in anything requires both talent *and* the inner drive and desire to succeed for your own sake. Most superstar athletes, when they were children, practiced and played on their own because they wanted to, not because they were forced by their parents or had a parent constantly looking on. In fact, the sports scene is littered with "fifteen-minute-fame phenoms" who were driven by overbearing parents and couldn't stay the course.

While it is important to encourage your children, their world won't come to an end if you sometimes miss a game or a performance. This is particularly relevant when a parent is ill, because one or both of you will not always be able to be there. So don't feel guilty. Go to their games and school activities when you can. When you can't, explain why honestly and let it go. If you have established good communication with your children, they will let you know if your absence bothers them, and then you can deal with it appropriately.

One of the greatest tragedies of our culture is the absence of extended family and neighborhoods and a sense of community. In the past, all of these provided a magnificent caring safety net when a spouse was ill or incapacitated. It was the most natural thing in the world for Grandma and Grandpa to take over, reassure the children, and provide them with the love, affection, caring, and discipline they needed. In addition, there was always an aunt or uncle or neighbor who automatically pitched in to provide the same warmth and affection. Today, however, most of us are down to the nuclear family, with few if any relatives nearby for support.

Children are incredibly resilient and will survive almost anything and will usually do so without making much of a fuss for a while. So it is very easy when you are worried about your wife's illness to forget the children if they are not under-foot and creating trouble. But just because they are not acting out doesn't mean they don't feel the stress of Mom's illness or that they are not internalizing it.

If you really want to love and care for your children, communicate with them and be there for them. Answer their questions. Reassure them. Meet their needs. This is the best way you can care for them and their mother.

CHAPTER

12

What about Sex?

During my junior year in medical school, one of my closest Christian friends was having some "problems." Although he was too embarrassed to go into detail, he did confide that he was going to see a urologist in the urology clinic. After he had been to the clinic, I asked him how it went. He said that he was more frustrated than ever.

"What's the problem?" I asked. "What did he say?"

"He told me my only problem was I needed to get a girlfriend and get laid."

My friend's "problem" was that he was sexually abstinent and chaste. He was a virgin! That in itself made him an exception in the clinic and certainly in the urologist's mind.

Chastity, abstinence, and faithfulness in marriage are foreign concepts in our culture. In the Bible, however, they are God's standards. In our sex-satiated society infidelity and promiscuity are so prevalent that they seem to be the norm. Yet I always go back to Ecclesiastes 1:9: "There is nothing new under the sun."

Clearly the Christians of the first century felt similar pressures, for the apostle Paul states in 1Corinthians 7:1–5:

> Now for the matters you wrote about: It is good for a man not to marry. But since there is so much immorality, each man should have his own wife, and each woman her own husband. The husband should fulfill his marital duty to his wife, and likewise the wife to her husband. The wife's body does not belong to her alone but also to her husband. In the same way, the husband's body does not belong to him alone but also to his wife. Do not deprive each other except by mutual consent and for a time, so that you may devote yourselves to prayer. Then come together again so that Satan will not tempt you because of your lack of self-control.

Sounds like Paul was writing to us, doesn't it?

Earlier when we talked about the differences between men and women, we acknowledged that there are obvious physical and emotional and, some believe, mental differences—differences, not superiorities or inferiorities. Clearly there are differences in sexual appetites and desires.

As a general rule, sex is more "important" physically for the male than for the female, while the intimacy and emotional aspects of sex often are more important to the female. This does not mean that we should separate the two, because sexual union is both physical and emotional. However, the two aspects can affect men and women differently.

A woman's monthly cycle and the resulting period is, in a sense, a release; this occurs whether or not she is sexually active. There is no such "automatic" release mechanism for a man from the sperm that is regularly formed in his body and the resulting pressure buildup. Most celibate men find release either in erotic dreams or nocturnal emission in their sleep.

One of the best ways to survive in this open sexual culture is to be married and have a regular healthy sex life with your spouse. There is little doubt that this is one of the best ways to avoid sexual temptation.

People who are sick or depressed, however, lose interest in sex. That is true of both men and women. The sicker you are or the more pain you are in, the less interest you have in sex, regardless of past experience. This can be a problem for the healthy spouse, who will still have his or her normal sexual interest and drive.

I vividly remember a made-for-TV movie a few years back about a woman who was stricken with multiple sclerosis and the struggles of this woman and her husband as she became progressively disabled. When she finally required full-time care, the husband hired a private live-in nurse.

Eventually the husband and the nurse had an affair. At the end of the movie, the completely disabled wife gave her permission and her blessing for her husband to leave her for the nurse because she could no longer fulfill his needs. The closing scene showed the husband and his lover leaving together as the disabled woman watched, bedridden and in a nursing home.

No mention was made about the immorality or wrongness of the husband's adultery and desertion of his disabled wife. The affair was portrayed as a thing of beauty, and the act of the disabled woman giving up her husband so that he could "be fulfilled and have his needs met" was portrayed as a generous and loving gesture.

That is our cultural mind-set: We all deserve to be fulfilled, our needs have to be met, and we deserve to have our needs met. And if our needs are not being met in our marriage, it is perfectly right and normal to have an affair. To do otherwise is unsophisticated and unenlightened.

In the book of Malachi, the prophet says, "Guard yourself in your spirit, and do not break faith with the wife of your youth" (2:15). Notice the phrase, "the wife of your youth." I see that reference as a reflection on one of the typical things that can happen when a woman becomes menopausal, and I believe that the Old Testament prophet was clearly warning men against leaving their wives for younger women.

As women get older, their estrogen levels begin to fall. When that happens, a woman may lose her desire for sexual activity. Another effect of falling estrogen levels is a physical condition called vaginal atrophy where the vagina actually shrinks and the lubricating secretions dry up. This condition can make sexual intercourse painful.

Now I don't mean to imply that all menopausal women lose interest in sex. Many, in fact, have renewed interest once the "fear of pregnancy" is gone. And menopause is not the only condition that can affect sexual activity. If you are sick, one of the first things you lose is your sexual appetite. If you are depressed, there is often loss of interest in sex.

So if your wife is sick, depressed, or going through menopause, chances are that at some point you will feel that she is not meeting your sexual needs. This is a common problem, but it is one men simply do not talk about! So most of us think we are the only ones going through this.

This is even more of a problem for Christian men who are committed to being faithful and honoring their marriage vows. So what's the answer?

Go back and read 1Corinthians 7:3–5 again:

> The husband should fulfill his marital duty to his wife, and likewise the wife to her husband. The wife's body does not belong to her alone but also to her husband. In the same way, the husband's body does not belong to him alone but also to his wife. Do not deprive each other except by mutual consent and for a time, so that you may devote yourselves to prayer. Then come together again so that Satan will not tempt you because of your lack of self-control.

The apostle Paul recognized that if married men and women abstain from sex for a period of time, Satan may use this as an opportunity for tempting them to fall into sin. I find it fascinating that the apostle—a bachelor—addressed this issue so forcefully and forthrightly and openly. The New Testament is not a sex manual, but Paul does talk about bodies, needs and desires, and marital duty.

So what are the biblical standards? What is the Christian to do?

First of all, you must talk about this matter openly and freely with your wife. It does no good to level accusations or make demands. You both need to honestly discuss your physical and emotional needs and desires. Talking about the difficulties you may be having, how you feel about them, and how she feels is the first major step to resolving the problem. Frequently that will be enough.

If not, and if some physical difficulty, illness, or surgery is creating a problem, the next thing both of you need to do is to be creative in fulfilling each other's needs. There are no biblical standards for you to meet other than to fulfill your "marital duty." There is no right or wrong way to do things, other than being loving and considerate and not being hurtful or distasteful to your partner. However, a good sex manual might be beneficial and helpful for you, even at this stage in your marriage—or maybe I should say *especially* at this stage in your marriage.

If your wife is going through menopause and is finding sex painful because of lack of natural vaginal lubrication, encourage her to consult her physician. The remedy may be as simple as one of the many good artificial lubricants that are now available.

Finally, you must accept the fact that when your wife is ill she just may not desire sex with the same frequency that you do. Conversely and ideally, she will accept the fact that you may need or desire sex more frequently than she does. (Again, some honest communication will help here.)

Sometimes, either because of her physical condition or her emotional state, your wife may be willing to satisfy you, but is passive in her reaction or may act or behave in such a way that it is obvious she takes no pleasure in this act or that there is nothing you can do to please her sexually. Don't consider that a rejection. There is nothing in the Corinthian passage, or anywhere else in the Bible for that matter, that says you both must have ecstasy and orgasm every time you have sexual relations. If you reread 1Corinthians 7 you'll find the words "duty" and "do not deprive." You won't find "Was it good for you?" in the Scriptures! Unfortunately, many of us have bought into the pagan Hollywood philosophy that says that sex has to be orgasmic and ecstatic and fantastic or somehow at least one of the partners has failed to perform.

The most important thing is for both of you to talk about your sexual relationship and mutually consent to fulfill each other's needs and desires in ways that are mutually satisfying. So TALK!

"But what do I do if my wife is so sick that any type of sex is totally out of the question?"

"What if my wife is so depressed that sexual relations are just not possible?"

There will probably be times in every marriage when abstinence is forced upon you. When it is, go back to 1 Corinthians 7, where the apostle recommends abstinence occasionally so you can devote yourself to "prayer." And observe his warning that Satan may tempt you.

I take great consolation in these verses and in 1 Corinthians 10:13:

> No temptation has seized you except what is common to man. And God is faithful; he will not let you be tempted beyond what you can bear. But when you are tempted, he will also provide a way out so that you can stand up under it.

In other words, others have been through it and survived, and so will you.

If your wife is so sick or disabled that no sexual gratification is possible, masturbation may be your only choice for release. Some of you may be shocked or offended by that statement, but that is the practical reality at times. Certainly I don't like to have to talk about that reality, but then I don't like the fact that anyone's wife is sick or disabled or depressed either.

Brother, let me reassure you, you don't have to feel guilty about it. Virtually every male has masturbated at some point in his life. It may very well be that God has provided this as a way out of temptation! No less an authority than Dr. James

Dobson has stated that we should quit railing against young men, teaching them that masturbation is sinful, when in fact it is normal. I have talked to missionaries, both theologians and physicians, who say that it is difficult enough to teach chastity and monogamy and faithfulness in other cultures, without the added burden of railing against masturbation.

While masturbation is a normal form of release, pornography is not. Pornography is sinful. It is of the devil.

First of all, pornography is going to change your relationship with God. That is what sin is.

Second, pornography will change your view of women. They will become objects of gratification.

Third, pornography creates unrealistic expectations, actions, and desires. It portrays women as things that want to be forced into having sex and only then will they enjoy it.

And finally, as a man thinketh so is he. These sinful thoughts will start to permeate your mind and eventually lead you into some type of sinful action.

Under no circumstances is pornography an acceptable form of release. It is sinful. It is going to harm your relationship with God, it will distort and affect your relationship with your wife, and it may lead you to have unrealistic expectations and demands and may even force her into doing things that she doesn't want to do or shouldn't do. And lastly, by purchasing pornography you will be supporting an evil endeavor.

"Rich, could I talk to you for a minute?" said Herb.

I had just finished leading a seminar at a men's retreat on "When Your Wife Is Sick" and Herb was one of the men attending the seminar.

As we walked down the hall to my room, he waited until everyone was out of earshot and then asked me, "What about masturbation? Is it okay? I need to have sex three times a week, and that is all there is to it. Unfortunately, my wife is only interested in having it twice a week. Those two times are very meaningful and wonderful, but if she is not interested I don't really want to impose on her and not have her enjoy it or be passive. In that situation, is masturbation okay?" he asked.

I told him that I felt it was fine in that setting as a form of physical release.

Herb had caught me offguard. This was one of the first times I had given this seminar, and I had not dealt with the issue of masturbation. I didn't expect the question and had not really thought it through carefully. If he were to ask that same question today, I would definitely qualify my answer.

In fact, as I wrote this chapter, I seriously debated about whether I should mention this subject at all. Some in the church consider masturbation sinful, and I do realize that my calling it normal is going to upset some people. Furthermore, I didn't want to become known as the doctor who suggested or supported masturbation. But I also knew that not to mention it would do my brothers, those of you who are struggling mightily and finding no release, a grave disservice. I wanted to alleviate any guilt feelings you might have in this regard.

The problem you need to be aware of is that masturbation can become habitual, and there are psychological problems with that. Also, if it is done to deprive your spouse of her marital rights, masturbation is spiteful and wrong. So I am not promoting this measure as much as attempting to reassure those of you who are in difficult circumstances.

If your wife is willing to be a passive partner in intercourse, that can be a very meaningful, loving act on her part for you. I would recommend that over masturbation. But that is different than forcing yourself on her if she doesn't feel good or isn't interested or if it is painful for her. Then you are better off abstaining. Only if you "must" have a release should you choose masturbation.

Remember, you are not alone. Many others have faced exactly these same problems before you. And no temptation is irresistible. You can trust God to keep the temptation from becoming so strong that you can't stand against it; He has promised this and will do what He says. He will show you how to escape and stand against temptation's power.

I believe sex is a bigger problem for Christians than for non-Christians. Not because we are obsessed with it, not because we are "puritanical," but because we strive to live by a higher moral standard—God's standard.

When illness strikes, it will affect this vital area of your relationship with your wife and may cause personal spiritual turmoil and temptation. I know it is tough, but God will see you through.

CHAPTER

13

What about Me?

It's a scene played over and over and over again at the end of the day.

Husband or wife comes home from work.

Wife: "How was your day? How did it go?"

Husband: "Same old stuff. How was your day?"

Wife then goes on for ten or fifteen minutes about the fact that her friend Jane is having marital troubles, the boss was sick, the air conditioning went out, your daughter's teacher called her from school because Mandy had a headache and needed Tylenol, and on and on.

I know that scene well. It is similar to those I live out almost every day of the week. Having been with patients and office personnel all day long I am "talked out," and since my day has been the same old routine, I don't really have anything interesting to say.

It's the kind of "conversation" that makes wives complain, "You never tell me anything . . . you never talk to me."

Much of the time they're right. We don't! But it's not that we men single out our wives for this neglect. We don't talk to our male friends either.

When we were single, we went out with the guys, shot the bull, or chewed the fat, or whatever you want to call it. We debated and argued, had fun together, chased girls together, and compared notes. "The guys" were our support group.

When we got married, we left all that behind. Some of it rightfully so, as we committed ourselves to our wives and our life together. However, many men also virtually cut off all lines of communication with their friends. Not only do they not hang out with the guys any more, they also don't talk to them any more.

When they are single, guys are proud of who they are dating and like to show off their dates. After they are married, men are proud of their wives and proud of their children and like to show them off as well. Typically, at least in a healthy marriage, a man's wife becomes his best friend—and she should be. If you marry your best friend or a woman who will become your best friend, that is ideal; that is the basis for a good, lasting relationship. Those are the marriages that work best. For many men, their wives also become their sole confidant for whatever they do share. Ironically, though, these guys often don't really talk to their wives either. In other words, they end up not talking to anyone!

In most churches, organizing a men's retreat is a major undertaking. It is difficult to get men to spend that much time together. Men's prayer breakfasts and Bible studies are often the most poorly attended functions in the church. The older men get and the longer they have been married, the more isolated they become.

Recently, however, we've begun to see this change. It used to be like pulling teeth to get guys to attend men's weekend retreats at our church. But slowly, as more and more men have participated in these events, they have come to understand the value of such interaction and have realized how isolated they were.

The great interest in the Promise Keeper movement is clear proof of the void that was there and the isolation men felt. There is no question in my mind that the power and success of Promise Keepers is that it has filled this huge void by providing opportunities for men to get together and share. Most men don't appreciate how isolated they are until they get together at a gathering like this.

The lifestyles we lead and the schedules we keep add to the problem. Between work and family life, there is little time left for anything else. So if your wife is your only confidant, what happens when she is sick? Who do you talk to then?

HAPPILY EVER AFTER?

As an Hispanic male, I was trained not to demonstrate or show weakness, not to show emotion. Grown men don't cry! Men don't show weakness. Men don't complain about anything. Did you ever hear John Wayne complain about anything? He could be shot in three places, have his grandson kidnapped, and he still never complained! That rugged frontier individualism is the ethic of the "macho" male. Solve your own problems.

In addition, many of us have been taught that the man must be the provider, the rock, the fortress, the protector.

Therefore, we conclude, if anything is wrong with our finances, our family, our marriage, our sex life, it is a direct reflection on us; somehow we have failed or messed up. And we can't let the other guys know there is something wrong because it is going to reflect badly upon us.

No guy wants to admit that he is having problems at home or that his wife is having problems or is sick, because deep down he thinks it is his fault and that he has done something wrong. If he complains about it, it will be even worse. He will be seen as weak or a wimp or a wuss!

Unfortunately most of us equate talking about something with complaining about it. *Communicating* about needs and problems is different than *complaining* about needs and problems, and we must learn to draw that distinction.

When a husband is sick or having problems, his wife usually has a best friend to confide in or an intimate circle of friends who will be her support group and with whom she can share her struggles. And because she has talked with other friends through the years, she probably knows that she is not the first woman to ever go through something like this.

When a wife is sick or having problems, however, her husband often has no close friend or support network. Furthermore, because we haven't made a habit of communicating on a personal level with other men, we tend to think we are the only ones who are going through this kind of struggle and that everybody else has perfect marriages and healthy wives.

Most of us grew up believing in the "happily ever after" of our childhood fairytales. In many ways, the church reinforced this in our minds. We were encouraged and admonished to "find just the woman God has for you" and told "what a terrific God-given institution marriage is."

Problem is, we are all fallen people. While God may have created marriage as a perfect institution, we are imperfect humans who have gotten married. And we do not live happily ever after. The romantic glow wears off and we realize that we are going to be living with each other forever. We make accommodations and compromises and accept little flaws and warts that we were totally unaware of. We discover things about our spouse that we didn't expect, and sometimes being married becomes a struggle.

Tied closely to the "happily ever after" fantasy is the myth that "once I am married, my sex life is going to be fantastic and my wife will be healthy and beautiful forever." Of course nothing in the Bible implies any of this.

God loves marriage; He created marriage. He wants us to be married, He wants to bless our marriages, and therefore He wants to bless our sex in marriage. But that is different than saying everything is going to be wonderful all the time and sex is always going to be fantastic.

Problems in marriage aren't new. If they were, why would the Bible speak so frequently against divorce? And the apostle Paul specifically instructs wives and husbands not to withhold their bodies from each other (1 Corinthians 7). These certainly are not the instructions one gives people who are having terrific sex all the time. Sexual frustrations in marriage are not new. Furthermore, there are going to be problems whenever your wife is ill (see chapter 12).

When "happily ever after" doesn't come true, we start to wonder what is going on because we have also bought into the idea that we "deserve to be fulfilled." That is one of the biggest lies our culture has foisted on us. If we aren't being fulfilled, then it is clearly somebody's fault. It could be your parents' fault or your boss's fault or your wife's fault—but clearly it is somebody's fault.

Chapter 13

Nowhere in the Bible do I find that we are promised emotional fulfillment, vocational fulfillment, or fulfillment in our marriage relationships. Instead, over and over the Bible talks about the spiritual warfare we are going to be engaged in. And if we are in spiritual warfare, Satan is going to try to attack us on every front, including marriage.

One of Satan's weapons is the pagan concept "I deserve." (This goes back to the Garden of Eden, where it was one of the implications underlying the temptation he offered Eve. "I deserve to know and have the right to know," thought Eve.) Satan implies that we have some innate right to fulfillment— whatever fulfillment means to us. And that's not biblical!

The third big lie we often hear, justifying all kinds of behavior, is that "God wants us to be happy." While God promises us His blessings, He does not promise us "happiness" our whole life long. Many people justify illicit relationships by saying, "I know God would want me to have this because my marriage is not happy and He wants me happy." This is not scriptural either.

The Bible does not say anywhere that God wants us to do things to make ourselves happy. God wants our obedience and our love and our worship of Him. He would never want us to do something that is sinful simply because it might make us happy. That is a seductive lie of Satan that our pagan American culture has adopted.

King David had tremendous bouts with depression; many times he was very unhappy. The apostle Paul sometimes sounds very depressed and downhearted; obviously he was not always happy. And it is certainly fair to say that Christ was sad at times because of the behavior of His followers and others.

Life has its ups and downs! Marriage has its ups and downs! God wants to bless us; He wants our lives to be filled with His joy and grace and peace. But nowhere does it say that God always wants us happy or that we are always going to be happy.

That fact becomes very evident, of course, when sickness enters the picture. Counselors say that the three great problems in marriage are money, time, and sex. When either spouse is sick, all three of these issues are going to be a problem. There are going to be financial stresses because if both of you work, as is common today, there is going to be a loss of income; even with insurance, illness costs. Time is also going to be a problem, simply because the well person is going to have more to do. And finally, when one spouse is ill, both persons are going to be deprived of sex.

At heart, however, I think the greatest problem in marriage is communication. When you analyze the problems over money, time, and sex, you begin to realize that at the root of most if not all of them is either poor communication or a failure or inability to communicate.

Which brings us back to why this is such a vital issue for men who are dealing with a sick wife. Most men have trouble communicating under the best of circumstances. So add in the stress of illness and you really get it between the eyes. In other chapters we've talked about various relationships that require communication—those with your wife, your children, your extended family, and your church. Here we want to talk about why communication is vital for *you*.

TAKING CARE OF YOURSELF

Your wife's illness is going to take a toll on you. She needs you now more than ever, but if you don't take care of yourself, you won't be able to be strong and healthy for her. You can't neglect yourself. You need help in handling the stress, particularly during a long-term or recurring illness.

You are going to need proper rest and relaxation and relief. If you think you don't, you are either deceiving yourself or you have a "codependency" problem; that is, your well-being comes from the need to care for someone. If the latter is the case, then you need counseling to help you address and deal with this unhealthy need.

"Stuffing" your feelings—denying or ignoring the fact that caring for someone who is sick is a stress upon you—is delusional and eventually leads to burnout and then anger over the frustrations you are experiencing and the total impact this is having on your life. That is a vicious cycle to get into: if you get angry about the situation or even angry at your wife because she is sick, then you are going to feel guilty because you are angry and that is going to exacerbate the problem and leave you empty.

If you want to be able to care for your wife, you are going to have to take care of yourself. If her illness continues for more than three or four weeks, you are going to need your own "R and R."

There are *three things* you must do to care for yourself so that you can better care for your wife, whether she is sick or healthy.

First, *establish a regular prayer and devotional life*. To be truly healthy, you need to be spiritually healthy, and that requires a diet of devotion and prayer. God has commanded us to pray to Him and to hide His Word in our hearts.

If you are not spiritually healthy, you will not be able to handle the stress of a long-term illness. Furthermore, you will be much better equipped to handle the normal stresses of married life and life in general if you have a regular devotional life.

A recent Gallup Poll showed that most men in America don't pray. This poll also indicated that the more money a man makes and the more education he has, the less he prays. Unfortunately, success can lead to a diminution of your prayer and devotional life.

I can't stress enough the importance of prayer and devotion and regular meditation. I believe that many of the problems we are having in our culture, the problems in our inner cities, the problems in suburbia, the problems in our marriages, the problems in our country, are attributable to one fact: the men in this country are no longer devoted to prayer and time with God. They have let their spiritual lives slacken and slip, and as a result they are plagued with narcissism, lack of commitment, adultery, and divorce. While prayer alone may not solve all problems, you are not going to solve any problems if you don't pray about them.

Satan has declared war on you and your marriage, and prayer is the most important thing you can do to win this battle. Without God's help, you cannot win; and to gird yourself in the whole armor of God, you must pray and meditate on Him.

You can't condition your body without regular exercise, and you can't condition your spirit without regular devotions. That takes a minimum of fifteen minutes daily. There are many ways to go about this, but if you're struggling with it, let me tell you what has worked best for me.

Buy a "one year" Bible. This is a devotional Bible that is laid out so that each daily reading includes a section from the Old Testament, the New Testament, the Psalms, and Proverbs; if you read each daily selection, by the end of a year you will have worked through the entire Bible. (These devotional Bibles are available in most of the major translations.)

Begin immediately to read the daily selection (you don't have to wait until January 1!) and pray every morning or evening, whichever is better for you. When you are meditating, think of the good things God has done for both you and your wife and for your family. Pray that God will enhance your love for your wife and thank God for her.

Form the habit of spending at least fifteen minutes a day on Bible study, prayer, and meditation. The tougher life gets, the more important it is to do this. And the more of a habit this becomes for you, the more important it will become for you. Prayer will change you, and it will change your relationship with your wife and with your children for the better.

God hears our prayers and will answer them, but He can't hear and answer if we don't pray.

The second thing you need is *regular rest and relaxation and exercise*.

God commanded the Israelites to rest one day in seven, and Jesus told His disciples, "Come with me by yourselves to a quiet place and get some rest" (Mark 6:31). That one day of rest is a very important principle—one the Lord himself observed during creation and instituted for us.

All of us need rest and relaxation. We will grind ourselves down if we don't have it.

As a physician, I frequently have to work on Saturday and Sunday; medical emergencies and illness don't wait for weekdays. Neither does crime or fire; police and firefighters must also work on the weekends. In fact, many occupations now require work on Sunday, but the Sabbath principle remains. We still need our one day in seven off. It is good for us spiritually and it is good for us physically.

Along with time for rest and relaxation, we need regular exercise. To be healthy, all of us need thirty minutes of regular exercise three times a week. By regular exercise I mean "continuous motion."

Walking is the safest, easiest, and least expensive form of exercise. If you walk at least thirty minutes nonstop three times a week, that is all the exercise you need for basic health. Some other alternatives are jogging, swimming, biking, running, racquetball, tennis, basketball, and aerobics. Do any of these with the same frequency: three times a week for thirty minutes nonstop—it has to be continuous to get the necessary affect.

If you want to stay healthy enough to care for yourself *and* your wife, make time for a regular exercise routine. While some may call women the weaker sex, the fact is that your wife will probably outlive you. She may see the doctor more often than you do during your lifetime together, but statistically she will live longer. One of the reasons is that most men don't get enough exercise.

Regular exercise will help you deal with the stress of her illness along with all the other stresses you have. Not only is it good for you physically, it is also good for you emotionally. Thus, it will make you a better husband and a better worker.

Just as a regular prayer and devotional life is essential for your spiritual health, so rest, relaxation, and exercise are essential for your physical and emotional health.

The third thing you need is *a friend—a male friend.* You need a good buddy you can talk to, and I don't mean a pastor or a counselor. You need a Christian tennis buddy, or a jogging partner, or a workout buddy, or a golfing friend, or a fellow basketball player, or a fellow walker, or a chess buddy.

Unless your wife is profoundly depressed and has totally cut herself off emotionally, I am going to bet that she has at least one good friend she talks to regularly, someone she confides in. I am also willing to bet that you probably don't. But you need to have a friend you can relax with, have a good time with, talk to, and confide in. This friend needs to be someone you trust. Someone you can really share your problems with—not just the basketball scores!

Above all, I stress the point that this should be a *male* friend. You cannot confide in a woman, single, divorced, or married. Don't tell your troubles to a woman other than your wife. And please don't think I'm being paranoid or overreacting here. This is dangerous territory, especially when you are the most vulnerable.

Talking about your feelings, your emotions, and your problems to a woman establishes a relationship between the two of you that you just can't let happen—no matter how seemingly "innocent" it begins. This is true even if the woman is the wife of one of your good friends or the wife of someone in your small group. The only time you can confide in someone like that is when her husband is present.

Now I'm not talking about a quick phone conversation or a brief discussion at work or at church, when you might be telling your friend's wife or an interested friend about a test result or how your wife's surgery went or that your wife is in the hospital. That's informational, and it's fine. I'm talking about you confiding in and sharing your deep feelings with a woman other than your wife.

This can be an even bigger trap or temptation at work. Many of us establish close and cordial relationships with our fellow workers. We're with them, elbow to elbow, at least five days a week and at least eight hours a day. Women are good listeners anyway, and when things are tough at home, it is easy to seek solace from such sympathetic sources. And believe me, there are plenty of single or divorced women, or for that matter married women, who will be more than happy to listen to you.

But here's the problem. First it's just talk. Then she becomes sympathetic and understanding, which is just what you've been looking for. And finally you begin to think that she really is the only one who understands. Once that happens you are hooked! Especially if you are sexually frustrated or deprived.

Believe me, Satan's timing is excellent. He will make sure that her sympathy hits you when you are feeling the most lonely or discouraged or deprived. And he'll use some ordinary woman who is easy to talk to and relate to—just a sweet, understanding person.

Casual sex and infidelity are so commonplace and accepted today that if you don't avoid such "innocent" conversations and dialogues, you will almost certainly be propositioned, either overtly or subtly. Or, what is even more common, you'll find yourself making such overtures. You may not have started out with the intention of prowling and propositioning, but deep down you may have that hidden hope that something more will come of it. If you want to get into a compromising position, believe me, Satan will make it very easy for you to do so.

Let me tell you, men, sex outside of marriage is easy to find. You have to be deaf, dumb, and blind not to find it, even if you are not looking for it. The problem is, it's sinful. God commands us not to do it. If you do, the consequences are far-reaching. It may well cost you your wife and family; it certainly will cost you a great deal of pain before you gain her trust back and any kind of restoration in your relationship.

The best preventative, of course, is to avoid putting yourself in the way of temptation.

GETTING SUPPORT

If you have a large and loving extended family and you get together frequently, you probably have brothers or other relatives you can relate to and confide in; if so, you are very fortunate. If you do not have a large family and you don't have any good Christian buddies, then talk to your minister or associate pastor or counseling pastor. There may be a support group for men in your church, or your minister can point you to a couple of other guys who are dealing with the same thing. (You'd be surprised how many people in your church are going through similar problems.) You can't do this alone; you shouldn't do this alone.

If you are not already in one, however, I strongly recommend that you get into a small group in your church. These are usually made up of four to seven couples who try to get together once a week or so for Bible study, prayer, and social time. We all need this kind of ongoing support, in sickness and in health. If you haven't already found it, there is no time like the present.

Small groups support their members with both prayer and actions. Galatians 6:2 says, "Carry each other's burdens, and in this way you will fulfill the law of Christ." Small groups answer this biblical imperative; they provide a network through which the church family can help each other when trouble comes.

The struggles we have been through in our own family have clearly demonstrated the incredible support network the Christian family—the extended family and the church family—provides. There is a reason God has told us to bear each other's burdens and to pray for each other. Our extended families and small groups are "battle groups" that help us survive spiritually, emotionally, and physically.

While you want to do what is best for your marriage and for your wife, it is not good for your marriage or for your wife to have a sick husband. You cannot devote all your energies to caring for her while denying that you have needs and stuffing your own feelings. Once I recognized this in my own life, it liberated me and I began to realize the importance of taking care of myself. I began to have the devotional life I needed, I quit depriving myself of appropriate rest and relaxation, and I sought out friends to talk to, so that I wasn't totally dependent on my wife for all of my emotional and social needs.

I don't mean that you just go off all the time and do your thing; but I do mean that you should not feel guilt and remorse about doing some of the things you need to do to keep healthy, even if you are doing them without your wife. There is nothing wrong with getting out one night a week for a golf game or a tennis match or a ball game.

In all fairness, of course, you both need rest and relaxation and time off. So if you play basketball one night a week and she stays home and baby-sits, then she is entitled to one night out while you stay home and baby-sit. If you work out at the gym three days a week, she is entitled to work out at her sport three times a week. If you go to a ball game once a month and she hates baseball or basketball or football, then make sure she gets to the theater or a concert or the movies or whatever she wants once a month. These are principles I am talking about, not score cards—but you get the general idea. Ideally, of course, most of the things you enjoy you'll be able to do together.

I'll never forget how crestfallen our pastor was at the divorce of a young couple in our church. They had gone through all the marriage counseling, were married in the church, seemed to be happy, but within eighteen months she divorced him because "marriage wasn't what she expected it to be." That is the exact opposite of commitment. When you commit to something, you don't bail out just because it is not what you expected it to be. You have committed to it, and now you have to make it work.

The Bible says that when a man and woman marry they become "one flesh." This is a very mystical but important concept. What it means here is that when one spouse is sick, both are going to suffer.

It's a bit like a car that has developed an oil leak: until that leak is fixed, it is more important than ever to check the oil and maintain the oil level in the car. If you don't, you will burn out the engine and wreck the car. The same can be said for our marriages. When one of us is sick, it is more important than ever to check the stress level and maintain our "inner workings." Depriving ourselves of the things we need to stay healthy is a bit like depriving that car of oil. It will have serious consequences.

If we are "one flesh," then we have to take care of both of us, not just one of us.

CHAPTER

14

For Better or Worse

Just watching Sheri Miller, it was apparent that she was depressed. She was wheelchair-bound, gaunt, and obviously very weak. She was suffering from multiple sclerosis, an unpredictable, illogical disease that can lead to total paralysis and death.

When Sheri became severely affected by MS, her husband left her and took their two children with him, according to the TV announcer. No wonder she looked depressed. The documentary on PBS, where Sheri's story was being told, was not about Sheri though; it was about her "doctor," a serial killer with an M.D., Jack Kevorkian. Sheri was one of Kevorkian's patients or victims, depending upon your perspective. He assisted her in taking her own life with his carbon monoxide suicide machine.

Illness brings pain and stress. A long-term, life-threatening, or terminal illness brings all this and more, and many people just can't handle it. And I'm not talking about the people who are ill; I'm talking about their spouses. Some break down emotionally. Some leave. I don't know Sheri Miller's full story, but I wonder if the ending might have been different if her husband and children had not deserted her. I have seen people much worse than Sheri, with a similar diagnosis, recover to the point where they have lived full and complete lives. Not often, but I have seen it happen. And in each case the person had the love and full support of his or her family.

If there is a problem in a marriage, be it the nebulous "incompatibility" or some severe stress, divorce is the first thing most Americans start to think about. It is the commonest option today—50 percent of all marriages end in divorce. But it is not the Christian option.

> Some Pharisees cae to him to test him. They asked, "Is it lawful for a man to divorce his wife for any and every reason?"

> "Haven't you read," he replied, "that at the beginning the Creator 'made them male and female,' and said, 'For this reason a man will leave his father and mother and be united to his wife, and the two will become one flesh'? So they are no longer two, but one. Therefore what God has joined together, let man not separate."

> "Why then," they asked, "did Moses command that a man give his wife a certificate of divorce and send her away?"

Jesus replied, "Moses permitted you to divorce your wives because your hearts were hard. But it was not this way from the beginning. I tell you that anyone who divorces his wife, except for marital unfaithfulness, and marries another woman commits adultery." (Matthew 19:3–9)

Now that is what Christ said. Not a lot of ambiguity there! Both the Old and New Testaments adamantly say that God hates divorce.

Divorce is not a new problem or a small problem or a rare problem. When things get bad and couples can't get along or the stresses are too great, divorce has always been one of the solutions (even in ancient times, according to the Bible). Divorce is the "easy way out"—even among Christians. Sadly, the rate of divorce among the churched and the unchurched, Christians and non-Christians, seems to be the same.

As we have already discussed, Satan is alive and well in America, and he has committed his forces to assault the American family; he will do anything he can to break up your family. Divorce is one of his favorite weapons. Unfortunately, in a divorce your children lose, your wife loses, and you lose. Only SATAN WINS!

THE PAIN OF DIVORCE

My generation was the one that really escalated divorce American-style. Remember the message we heard over and over again from those who were trying to justify getting divorced: "Children are much better off and will be much happier being raised by happy divorced people than unhappy married people"? This was reinforced by social workers, marriage counselors, and psychologists, all of whom thought the happiness of the parents was the most important element in raising "happy children"; honoring their marriage vows didn't even come into the picture. Men and women justified their selfish decisions with the claim, "Our constant fighting has to be worse for our children, and we will both be so much better off divorced and able to devote more time to our children."

Years later, we are learning how destructive all of this has been—and how misguided and just plain wrong. All kinds of statistics point up the problems children of divorce have.

The problem is, many people just don't want to work at anything that is difficult, and relationships that are lasting and mature are difficult and they take work. Yet the interesting thing is that children can benefit from seeing their parents work out their problems and differences, even if they do fight at times and are not always happy. Home is the place where children learn the values that will serve them the rest of their lives. So it is far healthier for them to see their parents stick together and struggle rather than doing the easy thing to try and make themselves happy. Through this, children learn that it is important to honor marriage vows.

All of this takes us back to an issue we discussed previously—the matter of happiness and fulfillment. One of the biggest cultural lies today is that somehow we can be happy (whatever that means) and fulfilled all the time, and it's usually at the expense of other people. God does not want us "happily divorced." God never wants us to violate His laws and recommendations.

The damage divorce does to children is a debate among some social scientists. There is no question that divorce is very stressful to children. Frequently they are psychologically damaged by divorce, and occasionally they are damaged quite severely. Children are torn between painful choices when their parents divorce. Sometimes children even blame themselves for the divorce; many of them think they did something wrong or failed in some way.

Remember, we said earlier that children are like tape recorders; they hear everything. Many times they hear things we don't want them to hear. But because of immaturity and lack of life experience, they are also terrible interpreters of what they hear.

Psychologists sometimes call this "magical thinking"— that is, the idea that somehow one's behavior could have changed the situation. These children think that if only they had been better kids, if only they had gotten better grades, if only they had made the honor society, if only they had been all-star basketball players, if only they had been queen of the prom, then their parents would have been proud of them and not fought and not gotten divorced. Many of these children think there was something they could have done to keep their parents from fighting, and then they wouldn't have divorced.

The reality is, of course, nothing children do or don't do causes a divorce or prevents a divorce. That is why it is called magical thinking. A child thinks, "If I had gotten A's, then (by magic) my parents would never have gotten divorced." That's like saying that the Bulls will never lose if I wear my Bulls shirt to the game; there is no relationship at all between the shirt I wear and the way the players perform. The same is true for children: no behavior or achievement of theirs can change their parents' relationship.

While psychologists and sociologists may debate the psychological harm of divorce, or lack thereof, there is no question that children of divorce pay a price. The present twentysomething generation, called "Generation X," is living proof. Unfortunately, "Generation X" is paying the price for the behavior of the parents of my generation. (Possibly that is one of the meanings of the "sins of the fathers being reaped by the second and third generations.") Forty percent of them are unmarried, whereas twenty years ago in the same age group, seventeen percent were unmarried. In 1990, for the first time in the history of the United States, there were fewer families formed than the year before. Even as I say this I think of Tony.

Tony is twenty-six years old. He works for an international corporation, and his career is going into orbit. For four years he dated Faith, a fine young woman who had her master's degree in special education and was active in our church. She came from a solid Christian home with loving Christian parents. Then, just as their relationship started to get serious, Tony began backing off; nine months later their relationship was over. Why? Because Tony was incapable of entering into a relationship that required commitment and trust.

Tony attended Christian schools and is a good Christian himself. But when he was in his senior year in high school his parents "suddenly" got a divorce. Both parents remarried, and in fact both couples are today on the mission field overseas. But Tony was so scarred by the breakup that he has admitted to his close friends and even to Faith that he just can't trust any woman enough to become involved with her.

Ernie Larsen, a popular psychologist on the talk show circuit, has said it best:

What you live with you learn.

What you learn you practice.

What you practice you become.

What you become has consequences.

Psychologists and social scientists are concerned by the increasing number of single young men, age twenty-five to thirty-five, still living at home with their mothers. Some call it the Peter Pan syndrome: these young men simply don't want to grow up. They don't want to make commitments. I believe at least one of the causes of this is the astronomical increase of divorce and the fact that these young people are failing to learn what a trusting, giving, mutually respectful relationship is.

Think of poor Sheri Miller's children and the lesson their father taught them. If Mom gets sick, dump her. Odds are—because I believe Ernie Larsen is right—that is what those children will practice and that is what they will become.

There is much, much more that could be said about the pain of divorce and the painful consequences, but there are already many books on the subject available. I merely raise the matter here because sometimes when things get tough, particularly when a spouse suffers from ongoing depression or mood disorders, some men are tempted to think that maybe it's just too hard and they should get out. For all of the above reasons and many more, that's not an option.

THE BIG QUESTION

"Why did I marry her?" Most of us have probably asked ourselves this question at some point. Certainly when I mention this in my seminars I've never had any man stand up and say, "I've never said that!"

It's one thing to ask yourself that question in a moment of discouragement. In fact, I think it's pretty normal. It's an entirely different matter to act upon it and say, "I'm getting out of this mess!" For better or for worse. Whether you said those exact words or not, you made that commitment when you married, and you vowed before God to keep it.

Actually, more than likely if you had it to do all over again, you would marry your wife again. I can almost guarantee it. You married her because of who she is, not in spite of who she is. So once you ask the question, "Why did I marry her?" you can begin looking at and gaining a clearer understanding of why you married her.

When we are young, we are prone to buy into the Hollywood concept of "romantic love," and we think that it's some romantic charisma or attraction that brought us together. While physical attraction can certainly be a factor in our initial attraction to each other, what keeps us together is much more likely an attraction based on both of our psychological needs and personalities so that there is a meshing that fits perfectly. The very specific needs and problems that she had are subconsciously what attracted you to her; and if you hadn't met her, you would probably have been attracted by someone with similar needs and traits.

All of us are familiar with the stories of women who are abused by alcoholic husbands. They eventually leave them or divorce them, swearing they'll never return or never get into that kind of relationship again. But they do; in many instances they return to their abusive husbands or they promptly marry other alcoholics who abuse them. It is not that they "need the abuse" or even want it. They don't. It is that meshing and subconscious attraction of their personalities that draws them together.

You married your wife because of who she is and who you are, and you need to face those issues. Because sometimes, of course, who we are can cause problems in a relationship, or can later contribute to depression or other mood disorders or even physical illness.

I have already mentioned that my wife, Judy, was raised in a home where alcoholism created the kind of psychological dynamics that typically occur in families where alcoholism is a problem. As I began to study codependency issues with my wife, I learned that we all send out invisible antennae or vibrations. Judy and I were best friends in college, and since we worked together in the dining hall, we ate meals together and talked regularly. We had fun together, and I truly loved her peppy, fun-loving spirit. I was also attracted to her vulnerability. I felt that she needed someone to care for her, although I didn't realize this until much later. She saw in me strength and stability—security—although I don't think she realized that until much later either. We meshed perfectly.

I am old enough that my children are starting to get married, my friends' children are getting married, and I have younger children who are doing a lot of dating. As this happens, it is interesting to watch who they date and who they choose to marry. Children typically choose someone like their father or mother. I had read this in many books on parenting and relationship issues, and my own observations have confirmed it.

Unless their home life is totally chaotic, traumatic, and disastrous, children tend to think home is the best place in the world to live, despite those years of teenage angst. With a few exceptions perhaps, their parents' relationship becomes the standard by which children judge and establish their own relationships. The children find a certain comfort level in the "chemistry" of their parents' relationship and the way they relate. Since it is the marriage relationship they have known close-up, they see it as the norm. When they begin to date, they feel comfortable or get "good vibes" dating those with whom they can relate in the same way that their parents related to each other. They feel comfortable and secure in that type of relationship.

To pick up on Ernie Larsen's philosophy, the home we live in is what we learn, what we learn we practice, what we practice we become, and what we become has consequences in our marriages.

Our children learn to be comfortable in the emotional environment in which they are raised. So when they start to date seriously and when they marry, they tend to seek out people with whom they get the same vibes and have the same comfort level that they felt at home. What they live with they learn, what they learn they practice, what they practice they marry.

I have seen this scenario repeated over and over again with my own children and with my friends' children.

My best friend is a great guy, but he has trouble saying no. He's a sucker for the downtrodden, people use him, and at times he borders on being a workaholic. He is also highly competitive in sports. The consequences of these traits bug his wife greatly at times, and she makes no bones about it. But their oldest daughter, in spite of intellectually knowing all this, married a young man who is just like her dad. In fact, her mother jokingly says that her son-in-law is so much like her husband that it's scary.

At times it is healthy to ask the question, "Why did I marry her?" First of all, because the answer is, "I'd do it all over again." And second, because it makes you address the issues in your life and the "problems" that you brought to the table in the first place. You need to remember why you were drawn to your wife in the first place, because she is still that person, despite the years and maturity and now the stress and illness. Those are issues the two of you need to discuss and address. (The same holds true from her perspective, of course, but in this book we're talking about you.)

Of course "Why did I marry her?" may require soul-searching if your wife is struggling with a mood disorder or a psychological or emotional problem. If she has an illness such as breast cancer, then the question should reinforce all the positives you saw in her. (Hopefully, those weren't purely physical.) As you recall these, you see the personality inside the body, because that personality is still there. That is what you have to remember and hang onto and love.

Dealing with this in an honest and straightforward manner will help you avoid another trap that is easy to fall into. When your spouse is ill, particularly with a continuing illness, it is easy to get high on the sympathy others may express to you because you are married to her. It may not be said quite this blatantly, but the implication is there: "Poor John. His wife is always sick." Or, "Poor John. It must be so trying for him dealing with her all the time the way she is. He is such a saint."

When things get bad, your *real* friends realize that things are tough and that you are struggling, especially if you are communicating with them honestly and asking them for support and prayer. This should not be done for the wrong motive though—to elicit cheap or maudlin sympathy. You ask for prayer because you need it (we all do), and people can't pray knowledgeably without the facts. Asking for prayer as a way to get sympathy is wrong. It is fine for friends to offer words of comfort and compassion and sympathy. It is very destructive for you to relish or revel in this.

Be thankful you have friends who are concerned about both of you. But remember, it is your wife who is struggling with the illness or the pain or the depression. Don't see yourself as the unfortunate long-suffering one who has to "put up with this." It is equally destructive for you to wallow in self-pity and think, "Oh, why am I suffering like this?"

This attitude can poison the atmosphere in your home and your relationship with your wife.

For your marriage to become a loving, mature relationship that can stand against and amid the storms of life, both you and your wife need to grow spiritually and emotionally. You need to have mutual respect for each other and not think of the other as the weak partner in the relationship.

When your wife is ill, especially with a lengthy or recurring illness such as chronic fatigue syndrome, diabetes, rheumatoid arthritis, or multiple sclerosis, your attitude toward her becomes crucial. You need to be like John, the missionary I mentioned at the beginning of the book, whose wife is totally disabled mentally by Alzheimer's disease. When friends tell John how sorry they feel for him because of the "burden he has to carry," John is emphatic in his response. He says from his heart that caring for his wife is no burden; it is an honor, because he remembers who she is. Caring for her is something he loves to do, and he means it!

When your mate is ill, you need to get beyond the physical and look at the psychological and emotional things that attracted you to her. Illness may have changed her in certain ways, but life itself does that to all of us! At times like this it is especially helpful to remind ourselves of God's love: He loves us no matter what we have done; He loves us in spite of our behavior, our actions, and our appearance. Being created in His image, we should ask for His strength and wisdom to do the same for the woman we have promised to love and cherish.

CHAPTER
15
How Can I Help
Her Get Better?

When I began my medical practice, I had a nurse named Faith. One day I had just finished examining and consulting with a patient who had been complaining of back pain. After she left, I told Faith that I could find nothing seriously wrong with the woman, and I was frustrated because there was nothing I could do or say that was going to help relieve her pain.

"Don't worry, Doc," she said. "She failed the faith test, and there is nothing you can do to get her better."

"What on earth is the faith test?" I asked.

"Actually, it's my own test," said Faith. She then told me that the woman had said to her, "Will the doctor tell my husband that my back pain will keep him from trying to have intercourse with me?"

When Faith heard those words, she knew that was the woman's agenda and that there was no way a doctor was ever going to be able to relieve her back pain. For this woman, hurting was better than being better because it kept her from having to do something she didn't want to do.

Pain clinics have a maxim: being pain-free has to be better than the pain or the patient is not going to get better. Motivation to get better has to come from within the patient.

I remember an occasion when one of my associates was very frustrated with one of his patients. He had performed a routine knee operation on this woman, and she still wasn't getting better. The patient was only in her fifties, and the surgery was such that within two to three months she should have been fully recovered. It had now been three months and she still wasn't making progress. Also, she had come in only once for the therapy required to aid in recovery after the surgery.

Months went by. The woman's husband refused to bring her in for therapy because he said that she said it was painful. He was pushing her around in a wheelchair and asking us to fill out forms that would entitle her to have a disability parking sticker. In fact, he wanted us to claim that she was "permanently disabled"—all this for a routine knee operation.

For the first couple months we willingly filled out the forms for the temporary handicapped parking, but it soon became obvious that this woman and her husband were quite content with her disability. Eventually, to try and encourage him to bring her in for therapy, we said that we would fill out the handicapped parking request on a temporary basis if, and only if, he brought her in for therapy and

she cooperated in therapy. We said we couldn't declare someone who should be fully recovered disabled. There was no
physical reason why she couldn't recover completely. When
we explained all this, the man became incensed and said they
would seek treatment elsewhere.

It was apparent that this man did not want his wife to
recover. What he really wanted was a convenient parking
place!

She, meanwhile, was enjoying the "secondary gains" of
her illness. She had her husband's attention (at least for the
present) and was making the most of it. There was no
motivation for her to get better.

MOTIVATION AND SUPPORT

Whether it is routine knee surgery or cancer, motivation
plays a major part in healing. I have been in practice long
enough to have seen many patients with similar or identical
conditions, so I have a pretty good idea of how long it takes
to recover from certain injuries or conditions. But while
physical healing may be predictable, emotional states are
not. That's why we often find that patients with work injuries
take twice as long to recover as patients who have the same
injury but did not get it on the job. Clearly multiple factors
enter into this, but I have discovered that motivation and
attitude about the injury play a significant role. In many
states, because of the tax laws, workers actually end up with
more take-home pay while they are injured. Also, frequently
workers are angry that they were injured on the job and
consciously or subconsciously want to punish their employers.

While we may do things that will inhibit someone from
getting well, as the man above did with his wife, the motivation to get better has to come from within the patient. If the

woman with the knee surgery had wanted to get to therapy, she would have found a way to do so. Part of recovery is the struggle to recover. If someone doesn't struggle or until they struggle, they may not get well.

Joni Eareckson Tada, the well-known writer and speaker, was an active athletic teenager until she dove headfirst into shallow water and ended up a quadriplegic. At first she lay in the hospital feeling sorry for herself, angry at her paralyzed state, and she did not make any recovery. Therapists helped her, pointed her in the right direction, guided her, encouraged her, but Joni had to do the hard work herself. The motivation for healing had to come from within her.

Joni has said that the turning point in her recovery came when she accepted her disability and decided she was going to get better and make the most of her life. She had to motivate herself to begin her recovery; nobody could do it for her. Today she paints, writes, has her own radio program and ministry, is happily married—and drives her own van!

The same is true for the person who has a broken ankle or is recovering from abdominal surgery or any other type of illness. If your wife has a broken ankle and you don't ever let her use her crutches but push her around in a wheelchair and wait on her hand and foot, you are not really helping her. If she is not forced to do things for herself, her recovery is going to take much longer. I don't mean you should be cruel or lazy or neglectful, but remember that the struggle to do things for herself improves or speeds up your wife's recovery.

Mary was a beautiful and talented woman. She came from one of the "best families" in town. In college, she started to enter beauty contests and eventually won the Miss America pageant. She married and had two beautiful children. Then she began to develop all kinds of stress-related illnesses. Her first marriage ended in divorce. She married a second time, but that marriage was stormy as Mary continued to be plagued with multiple illnesses.

Then her father, a pillar in the church and the community, died. After his death, Mary started undergoing psychotherapy, and it became apparent that she had been sexually abused by her father. She had been repressing that fact and could not even confront it herself until after her father died. Later she learned that her sister had also been abused. Mary's stress-related illnesses were the consequence of that suppression.

Meanwhile, however, her husband was having difficulty even believing her. He had liked his father-in-law, so he questioned Mary's allegations. Once he realized the truth, his support and encouragement became an integral part of her recovery.

Joan is a nurse for one of my physician friends, and I had treated her for over ten years for upper back and neck pain. The diagnosis was fibromyalgia, a painful stress-related illness.

One day, after I had not seen her for a couple years, Joan came for an appointment, and as I talked to her and discussed the diagnosis and the relationship of her pain and symptoms to stress, Joan broke down and started to cry. She then told me that she had been sexually abused as a child and had recently begun dealing with the fact. The current stress came from the fact that she was going home for the holidays to visit her parents. She was trying to decide whether or not she was going to confront them. Her husband was so angry about what her father had done that he was *demanding* that they confront him about it!

When you hear the statistics on the number of children who have been abused sexually or hear about the incidents of incest in our country, you may have trouble believing it is that prevalent. I know that I did. Yet I now believe the statistics. My experiences as a physician, the things I have learned as an elder in the church, and some of the "family secrets" I have learned from our large extended family have all convinced me, and it makes me angry and sick at heart. I look at my lovely daughters and cringe at the thought of a father doing something like that to his daughter. And it is happening in "Christian" homes.

As in Mary's and Joan's cases, it is common to find stress-related illnesses that are a result of repressed childhood events. Incest is one of the worst. Frequently it takes the death of the guilty parent or relative for a child to even admit that it happened or come to grips with it. And the worst thing you can do, if your wife tells you that this happened to her, is not believe her. You can't begin to imagine the pain and the enormous struggle it has been for her just to admit to herself and then to you that it happened. The most devastating thing you can do to her is to deny the reality of what she is telling you by saying, "No way. I know your father. He's a good guy. He is not capable of that."

You have to respect your wife and what she tells you. You have to encourage her to work through this and to talk to you about it. You have to accept the fact that it happened and you have to accept her; you cannot look upon her as "damaged goods." You have to love and support her. Admitting this has happened is only the beginning of a long struggle for her, and you are going to have to allow her time and "space" to heal. You can help her recover by doing all of the above, but ultimately she has to work through this herself.

After the initial shock and disbelief, your response may very well be anger. It is normal to be angry that someone did this to the woman you love. But you must not confront the offender. If you do, he is most likely going to deny it. When to confront the offender or whether to confront the offender must be your wife's decision. It may be that she will never do so. Whatever her decision, you have to support her.

If the parent or relative who abused her is still living, family get-togethers may be very difficult and painful; in fact, the two of you may decide to avoid them as much as possible or curtail them altogether. Now you understand why in the past she has been reluctant to go to family gatherings. And remember that her brothers and sisters may not have come to grips with this, even though it is highly likely that some if not all of them were abused as well. They might even deny that it ever happened. Don't force her into socializing with them if she doesn't want to, nor should you pressure her into forgiving the abuser and the family, especially if the family hasn't admitted that this happened or could have happened. You don't know what this has done to her, and you don't know what you are truly asking her to do. While forgiveness is certainly admirable and Christian, it takes a great deal of time to work through trauma like this and truly forgive someone for this type of abuse.

Victims of incest frequently suffer from anxiety attacks or stress-related illnesses. For years they may have suppressed their anger and pain. Frequently they feel inferior, and psychologists will tell you that they fear success. Often they hate themselves; as a result, some of their behavior may be self-destructive. The biblical standard is to love others as you love yourself. Yet victims of abuse have trouble liking or loving themselves. All of these things lead to difficulty with intimacy and the ability to give and receive love in a relationship—spiritually, physically, and emotionally. If your wife was sexually abused, she may well have trouble with intimacy in your relationship. This, too, will take time.

If your wife is struggling with traumatic issues from her childhood, I strongly recommend that you read *Love Is Not Enough* by Drs. Minirth and Meier. If she is coming to grips with these matters, then clearly she is motivated to face up to them and get better. You can help her by being committed to her, by letting her know that you are going to be there for her, that you are going to go through this with her, and that you will support her all the way.

As your wife works through this trauma from her past, she may want to start attending a support group. Watching your wife become more independent and start "doing her own thing" can be scary, but you need to step back and let go. Many support groups are now being sponsored by and held in churches, and if she can find one like that, it would be an advantage. (Some support groups have a New Age bent, and some even encourage divorce.) Nevertheless you still have to back off and let your wife get better on her own.

Meanwhile, be sure *you* support *her* strongly in prayer. Pray for her and with her and request prayer from your own "support group." While this isn't the only key, it is key.

If alcoholism is your wife's problem, the right kind of support is just as crucial. You need to support her, but you must not support her addiction or problem. You need to love her, but you don't want to do anything that will help her stay addicted. You have to let her come to grips with the problem herself and with the consequences of her behavior. If you don't, you are an "enabler." In other words, you "enable" her to continue her destructive and self-destructive behavior. The best thing you can do is let her wake up in the morning and see the mess she has created.

Remember the rhinoceros in the living room? One of the biggest problems in families where there is an alcoholic is that truth is one of the first victims. The entire family is taught to deny that there is a problem. And should anyone outside learn the truth—which often happens in the case of alcoholism—the spouse is portrayed, by self and others, as the long-suffering Christian wife or husband.

Another aid to motivation is something called "intervention." The key to successful intervention is having a professional help you. This professional will gather together the family members who are willing to cooperate as a group to confront the impaired person regarding the consequences of her alcoholism or other addiction and the effect it is having on her family and herself. This has to be done well and in such a way that the consequences of the alcoholic's actions are seen and cannot be refuted. One person confronting an alcoholic or an addicted person is going to be greeted by denial, which is one of the symptoms—denial that she has a problem, denial that she can't control her drug or her alcohol or her behavior. So one-on-one confrontation is not going to be successful. As a group the loved ones describe what it is like when the person is drunk.

If alcoholism or addiction is your wife's problem, the worst thing you can do is cover for her, make excuses for her, and lie to your children about her behavior. The loving thing to do, the Christian thing to do, is to tell the truth.

THERAPY

Support groups are one thing. Therapy is something totally different. Support groups do not do therapy. So if, as the result of past traumas or other problems, your spouse is suffering depression or anxiety, she may well need some kind of counseling or therapy from a psychologist or psychiatrist. If medication is indicated then she will need the latter because psychiatrists are M.D.'s and can prescribe medication for depression or manic depression or anxiety. If your wife needs therapy to help her get well, encourage her to get it and then support her.

In the past, many Christians have been fearful that seeking such help would be seen as a lack of faith, or that their faith itself would be seen by the "experts" as a sign or cause of mental disorder. Today, fortunately, most people realize the value of counseling or therapy in certain situations, and there are also many Christian psychiatrists and psychologists. My feeling about Christians in this profession is the same that I have regarding other physicians and practitioners, especially when it comes to mood disorders and psychiatric and psychological issues: I think it is preferable for a Christian to see a Christian psychiatrist or psychologist, but I no longer believe it is essential because good psychiatrists and psychologists now acknowledge that religion and faith can be and are an important part of a person's mental and physical well-being. No competent therapist is going to impugn your faith or blame your problems on your religion. If one does, then you need to see a different therapist!

Therapy, however, is expensive, which is an added stress for most of us. So you and your wife need to sit down and count the dollar cost of therapy and commit to that. Insurance will cover some psychotherapy, but on the newer insurance forms, unless you have a platinum plan, there is a restriction on the number of visits the policy will cover. Most people have to pay some out-of-pocket expenses.

If your wife's psychiatrist suggests or prescribes medication, both of you need to be informed of the name of the medication and any potential side effects. All of these "mood-altering" medications have side effects. Having said that, I would also reassure you that most of these medications are fairly safe and the side effects are more annoying than serious. Tricyclic antidepressants, for example, are known to cause a dry mouth and urinary retention (difficulty in emptying the bladder). Occasional muscle cramps and itching are two other common side effects.

Ask your physician or therapist for a summary sheet of the side effects and the expected benefits, and ask how long it takes for the medicine to work. Many of these "mood-active" or "mood-altering" drugs take two to three weeks to start showing any effect. Your wife may also be dealing with the effects of female hormones, so it may take a calendar (the kind we have talked about in previous chapters) to sort out the effects of the medications. Both of you need to keep a calendar: on hers, your wife needs to record how she is feeling and any changes in her mood while she is taking the medications; on yours, you need to record your honest perception of how she is doing. The key word here is "honest," because this information is vital in gauging the effectiveness of the medication. Also, after being on a medication for some time, she may develop new side effects and a change may be needed.

Even if medication is prescribed, this does not mean your wife will have to be on it permanently. Occasionally that is the case, but often the person needs the medicine for a period of time and then is able to come off it or at least move to a lower dosage.

There is no question that those with mood disorders have altered brain chemistry. While it is not clear which came first—the altered chemistry or the disorder—there is no question that the treatment of mood disorder has been one of the great advances of psychotherapy and psychopharmacology in the past decade. These mood-active drugs can be very effective, but they also affect each person individually and differently to varying degrees. That is why open and honest communication is so important. You need to affirm how your wife is feeling and how she is acting and validate her responses so that she "won't think she is crazy."

And don't let the old "lack of faith" accusation keep you from seeking this remedy. Taking such medications does not demonstrate a lack of faith any more than taking antibiotics for an infection or insulin for diabetes demonstrates a lack of faith.

TEN COMMANDMENTS

While you cannot "make" your wife better, your support can be crucial in bolstering her own motivation and ability to heal. So here are my ten commandments for you—things you can do to help her get better.

First commandment: *Hug your wife at least once a day.* And I don't mean a perfunctory hug; I mean a bear hug where you hold onto her tightly for a while.

Frequently, hugging communicates much more than words. Some cardiologists feel the predictor of whether a man will survive a heart attack or not is whether he hugged his wife in the previous twenty-four hours! Premature babies can have the best and most modern technological care, they can get the right drugs and all the right treatment, but if they are not hugged and rocked, they won't survive. That is why you will always see rocking chairs in preemie nurseries, and why nurses are encouraged to rock the babies whenever possible. When nurseries are short-staffed or when there is no parental involvement with the child, hospitals will ask for volunteer grandparents to come in and rock babies.

Holding and hugging is powerful, healing medicine. Practice it at least once a day.

Second commandment: *Hold her hand and touch her daily.*

If your wife is hospitalized in critical condition with tubes and apparatus or if she is in a serious infectious state, you may not be able to hug her. But there is almost no condition that would prevent you from touching her and holding her hand.

Touch is powerful, powerful medicine. The big criticism of modern medicine is that it is high-tech and low-touch.

Christ used touch in many of His miracles. He touched the eyes of the blind, He touched the deaf, He touched those who were paralyzed. He even touched lepers, which was taboo in the culture of His day. He touched them all with His healing love.

Third commandment: *Kiss your wife every day.*

You need to show her some love and affection every day.

Fourth commandment: *Pray for her daily.*

Over and over in the New Testament we are commanded to pray for one another. Prayer is potent medicine. You are depriving both of you of an essential healing power if you do not pray for your wife.

When you pray for her on a regular basis, you will be reminded of all the other practical and proactive things you can do to aid in her recovery. Prayer changes things.

Fifth commandment: *Pray with her.*

We are also commanded to pray with one another. The Bible says where two or more are gathered together, there Christ's presence and the Holy Spirit will be. Hold her hands or put your arm around her while you are praying with her.

Praying together will also help the two of you communicate better. Prayer works.

Sixth commandment: *Ask others to pray for her.*

Ask your church, your Sunday school class, your Bible study or prayer group, and your small group to pray for her. If you have Christian families, ask them to pray for her, although they are probably already doing so. Ask your Christian friends to pray for her.

Some people are very private people and have difficulty sharing their personal concerns. I understand that. Yet the Bible commands us to share one another's burdens and to pray for one another, and people can't pray for us if they don't know there is a problem or if they don't know how to pray and what to pray for.

There is great spiritual power in corporate prayer. The Bible says that!

The older I get and the more experience I have, the more convinced I am of the power of prayer and its healing effects. It amazes me how few people pray for God to guide the wisdom of their physicians and surgeons, or that they might be spared the side effects of medicine or chemotherapy. Several times when I have had to perform serious operations, family and friends have committed to pray for me as a surgeon while I operated on their loved one. Each time, these severe, difficult cases went better than I could have ever dreamed they would have gone.

Prayer can make a good surgeon brilliant—and keep brilliant surgeons out of trouble!

Pray for your wife's physicians, surgeons, or therapists, and ask others to pray as well.

Seventh commandment: *Commit to her!*

I implore you to tell your wife that no matter how sick she is, no matter how long this has gone on, no matter what she looks like, no matter what you have been through, no matter how she is acting, you are committed to her and committed to your marriage and that you are going to stick together through this time of trial and suffering. With God's help you are both going to pull through this and as a result your marriage will be even better.

If your wife has been sick or depressed for a long time and has been less of a wife to you than you think is fair, I can assure you she is aware of that. There just may be nothing she can do about it. She may not even have the energy to face it. But even though she may not act like it or say anything, she may be afraid that you are going to leave her.

If that is the situation, tell her you are not going to bail out of the marriage. Fear that you are going to leave her can paralyze her and stop her from doing some of the things she needs to do to get better. No matter how irrational these fears may be, they are very common.

Continually let her know that you are committed to her and to your marriage. Of course, you can't be lying or two-faced about this. You have to be committed to the marriage and committed to her.

Eighth commandment: *Tell her not to worry about her appearance.*

Appearance really is only skin deep. Tell her that no matter what she has lost, it hasn't changed your love for her. If she has lost her hair, or a breast or both breasts, or now has a huge scar, she is going to fear that she has become unlovely and unlovable, unattractive or unfeminine. Such thoughts may have never crossed your mind, but you must verbalize to her that her appearance doesn't matter.

If you don't mean it, of course, then you have a problem yourself. If what she has lost is important to you, then you are going to have to face up to that and work through it. If your wife's losing a breast or her hair totally turns you off or worse, then you have some problems you need to address and you'd better get some counseling yourself.

Now you may be seeing why it is important to hug her, hold her hand, and kiss her. You can say all the "right words," but if you stand back, stand off, or are repelled by her appearance, she will pick up the signs and signals. She will read your body language and not hear a word you say.

Ninth commandment: *Get REAL!*

While psychologists coined this term, "getting real" applies to all illnesses.

R is for respect. You have to respect what your wife has been through.

E is for encouragement. You have to encourage her in every way you can, encourage her to get better, encourage her to do the things she needs to do to get better.

A is for acceptance. You have to accept her for what she has been through and for who she is now.

L is for listening. You have to listen as she talks about how she feels.

Half of communication is listening. Listening to someone who is sick is one of the hardest things to do. But she needs to verbalize; she needs to talk about how she feels. This can be difficult, painful, frustrating, and even boring, but it is very important that you show her respect, encourage her to talk, accept what she is saying, accept her, and listen to what she has to say. (Remember, psychiatrists get paid for doing that!)

Listening is very therapeutic.

Tenth commandment: *Give her the freedom to die!*

"Hey, wait a minute!" you may be saying. "What's going on here? We've been discussing how to help my wife get better and suddenly you're talking about dying?!"

Cancer surgeons can tell you story after story of patients who continue to undergo disfiguring or excruciatingly painful treatments or chemotherapy, even when the situation is hopeless and there is little chance that the therapies will help. Yet the person continues to fight because his or her loved ones won't "let go."

There does come a time in all of our lives when we are going to have to die. Depending on circumstances and age, this may not seem fair and it may not make sense. But if the outlook is hopeless and your loved one is only undergoing the treatment because you won't let go, you need to give her the freedom to die. You need to be able to say, "Honey, I love you, I don't want to lose you, I don't want you to die, but this isn't working. I hate to see you suffering with all these treatments. You don't have to keep doing this for me. I am going to support you in whatever decision you make. But please don't keep doing this to yourself just because of me. If you want to stop all these miserable treatments or not go ahead with this surgery, I understand. Modern medicine has nothing more to offer us."

If her illness has progressed even farther than that and it is clear to everyone that this is the end, you need to be able to pray for her suffering to end and to say, "I'll see you on the other side, sweetheart. I'll see you in heaven."

Ultimately there is nothing we can do to motivate someone to want to get better. That has to come from within the person. We can, however, provide a good environment and enough love so she wants to get better.

Recovery from most illnesses tends to be a bit like the stock market: there are ups and downs. On the road to health and wellness there are peaks of progress and ravines of relapse. This can be very frustrating and stressful for both of you. But God is faithful; He has promised to see you through the valley of the shadow of death. Don't despair. Hang in there.

CHAPTER

16

Can I Expect a Miracle?

"Can I pray or *should* I pray for a miracle?"

"Can I expect a miracle?"

Many Christians may be reticent to ask these questions out loud, but I'd venture to say that all of us have asked them internally at one time or another.

When people start talking about miracles, the first verses they usually go to are James 5:14–16:

> Is any one of you sick? He should call the elders of the church to pray over him and anoint him with oil in the name of the Lord. And the prayer offered in faith will make the sick person well; the Lord will raise him up. If

he has sinned, he will be forgiven. Therefore confess your sins to each other and pray for each other so that you may be healed. The prayer of a righteous man is powerful and effective.

These verses can be interpreted in many ways—and have been. Entire books have been written on the subject. There is no way we can delve into an in-depth discussion of healing, nor is that our purpose here. What I want to focus on is the matter of miracles and miraculous healing.

The major thing I notice in these verses is that nowhere does it say that the sick person will be *miraculously* healed or even that the sick person will *always* be healed; it doesn't even say that we will be healed in this life.

What it does say is that we are to pray over a believer who is sick. To bring it down specifically to our topic: if your wife is sick, you should ask the elders or leaders of your church to pray for her and anoint her with oil. If your church elders will not do this, then you need to seriously look at the theology of your church.

Notice that this passage does not say these prayers should be offered at a healing service or even at a public service. My view is that this should probably be a private service with just your wife, the elders, and you present.

While the setting or the meeting place is not defined, however, it is clear that there is no place for unconfessed sin in a prayer for healing. If you and your wife do call for the elders to come and pray over her, expect to be questioned about any unconfessed sin; clearly your sin must be confessed and forgiven before the prayer for healing is offered. Prayers for confession and forgiveness of sin must precede the prayers for healing!

Having said all of this, though, we still ask, "What about expecting a miracle or praying for a miracle?"

Personally, I do believe in miracles. Miracles can and do happen. But as Nigel Cameron, the British theologian, says, "The God of the abnormal is also the God of the normal."

Some extreme views contend that we should always pray for miracles and not seek any medical treatment. But if we believe in miracles, then we also should be able to believe that God can use modern medicine. Dr. Cameron says there is no theological justification for not seeking medical treatment. In light of that, he maintains, we need to look at the context of the miracle.

One of the appropriate places to look for miracles, says Cameron, is in people whom medical treatment or science has failed. We should pray for the sick, lay hands on them, use a doctor, and seek God's will. His other exhortation and, if you will, disclaimer is a reminder that "we are mortal." If everyone was healed of every illness every time, none of us would die!

Also, he reminds us that there is no biblical support for some specific process that will always lead to a miracle. In other words, we can't manipulate God. If it is miraculous, it is equally unpredictable. We are to seek the Lord's will, but we can never forget that it is *His* will, not ours.

I believe we can pray for miracles and expect them to happen. But here's the interesting question: What is a miracle? There is no simple definition. In fact, it's hard to get any two theologians to agree on a definition, and many Christians disagree about miracles. I am sure you, too, have your own idea or definition, but let me give you some things to consider.

WHAT IS A MIRACLE?

In my reading and study, I have been able to come up with at least a dozen definitions or different types of miracles.

These are not all-inclusive nor are they listed in any order of importance or validity—with the exception of the first.

The miracles Christ performed

Instantly, with His word or touch, Christ cured people who had infections, heart failure, blindness, speech impediments, demon possession, seizure disorders, paralysis, scoliosis and spinal deformities, or leprosy. (Leprosy is a disease that causes permanent scarring and loss of body parts, and Christ cured lepers so completely that their deformities and scars were gone.)

Christ also raised the dead. His friend Lazarus had been dead for days when Christ raised him.

By any criteria you use, these were miracles. What Christ did defied the laws of medicine and physiology. He restored dead tissue to full wholesome life; in fact He even recreated tissue. He defied the then-known laws and rules of science and medicine and all the currently known rules and laws of science and medicine. These were signs to the people of His day who saw them as well as to us who read about them.

Furthermore, these miracles were prophesied in the Old Testament. We must not forget that Christ's miracles were a fulfillment of prophecy.

The most important thing to remember, however, is that Christ claimed that His miracles were proof that He was equal to God, that He was the Son of God. He also said they were a result of faith and prayer.

What Christ did was miraculous. No other miracles meet the gold standard of those He performed.

The miracle of modern medicine

Many of the conditions Christ treated—conditions untreatable in that day and age—can be treated by modern medicine. Infections are treated with antibiotics; heart failure with digitalis; female bleeding with a relatively minor surgical procedure; leprosy can be prevented and treated with antibiotics and surgery; some types of blindness can be treated with cataract surgery; some types of deafness can be treated; many orthopedic deformities are correctable; certain types of paralysis can be treated; and at times we can even cheat death for a while with CPR.

We should not negate or depreciate the value of modern medicine. Christ said the sick need a doctor, and the apostle Paul chastened Timothy for not taking wine as medicine for his stomach (Matthew 9:12; 1 Timothy 5:23).

"An uncommon, often unexpected event in a physical, chemical, or psychological system that cannot be attributed to a known physical, chemical, or psychological force"

This definition comes from Dr. John R. Brobeck, the Herbert C. Rorer professor in Medical Sciences at the University of Pennsylvania. The problem with this definition is that the quality or the size of the miracle or whether something is a miracle depends on your scientific knowledge or sophistication.

Dr. Brobeck seems to imply that if we had enough knowledge, we would be able to understand all miracles. Thus, things that some of us accept as miracles others see simply as ignorance of scientific data or facts. One man's miracle is another's expected scientific occurrence. By this definition, the less scientifically informed you are, the more miracles you are going to see.

In the early days of medical missions, Christian eye surgeons who were experienced in cataract surgery would donate their services to mission hospitals for a period of time. The missionaries would line up the patients, and these surgeons would perform cataract operations from morning to night for several weeks. To these third-world people, successful cataract surgery was miraculous because the blind were made to see. Some of the early success of mission hospitals was directly attributed to the high success rate of cataract surgery, alleviating blindness for many people.

Spontaneous remission

Spontaneous remissions are known medical phenomena. In the midst of progressive deterioration, when all treatments have failed, certain tumors and illnesses have been known to spontaneously get better for no known explanation at all. (*Remission* means that the tumor or illness has gone away and there is no evidence of it in the body anywhere.)

I'll never forget the head of a Baptist mission organization describing the case of a young executive with a widespread lymphatic tumor who had been sent home to die. All treatments had failed; the situation was hopeless. Having been told by the medical establishment that there was nothing further they could do, the man's family took him home, fully expecting him to die. To make a long story short, fifteen years later, having had no further medical treatment, the young executive being described in the story was the head of the Baptist mission organization!

The man then went on to describe his frustration with the medical establishment because they told him that his healing was not miraculous; in fact they argued with him! They told him the tumor he had was known to occasionally have spontaneous remissions that were totally unexplainable; his was not the first case.

There is no good medical explanation for spontaneous remissions. They are just accepted as one of the things that certain types of diseases occasionally do. Certain types of cancers as well as neurological diseases are notorious for spontaneous remissions. They can be defined as miracles if they happen to you or a loved one you have prayed for, but jaded physicians will dismiss that definition, saying, "It was just a spontaneous remission. It was not miraculous at all."

Are spontaneous remissions miracles? Are they an answer to prayer? I guess it depends on your perspective. As far as I'm concerned, they certainly meet many of the criteria or definitions of a miracle.

Happy coincidences

Before 1968, Rh incompatibility was a scourge of new-born babies. If you and your wife were Rh incompatible, then it was probable that some of your children would have Rh incompatibility between their blood and your wife's blood. This could be lethal for newborns.

All of us are either Rh positive or Rh negative. One of the reasons blood typing is done before a blood transfusion is so that a patient isn't given the wrong type of blood; otherwise, the immune system will attack those incompatible "foreign" blood cells and lead to what is called a transfusion reaction.

So if you and your wife were Rh incompatible, this could lead to an immune disease situation where your wife's blood cells would attack your child's red blood cells, leading to severe anemia and jaundice. Frequently this would require extensive "exchange transfusions" where they would totally exchange blood from your child. This could severely damage or even kill a newborn child.

My wife and I always wanted to have a large family, but before we even began to have children we found out that we were Rh incompatible. As a resident in training, I was fully aware of the medical problems but was not really that current on the new advances in research on Rh incompatibility. My wife, however, began to read voraciously on the subject and learned that there was a new technique and that it would soon be available to the public.

Three weeks before the premature birth of our oldest child, Jennifer, the FDA released RhoGAM, an injection that would prevent Rh incompatibility. Jennifer and Judy are Rh incompatible, so the injection was vital. Judy was one of the first people in the Chicago area, if not the first, to be treated with RhoGAM. To us, that "happy coincidence" was an answer to prayer and our own little miracle.

Many theologians are quite content to define happy coincidences as miraculous.

"Extraordinary intervention by a supernatural power, either God or Satan"

That is how several theologians I have read define a miracle. They usually use terms like "breaking through" the laws of nature to describe such interventions. In other words, a miracle is something that defies natural law. Not only can it not be explained, but it goes "counter to the laws of nature."

Most people agree that something that goes counter to the laws of nature is the best definition of a miracle. Certainly the miracles Christ performed went counter to the laws of nature. People who have been dead for four days, as Lazarus was, can't be restored to life and health by any known laws of nature. In fact, that miracle defies everything we know about science and physiology.

Yet some excellent theologians are "troubled" by this definition. First of all, they are troubled by the idea of "breaking through the laws of nature." These are laws that God created in the first place, and they are troubled by God "breaking" His own laws. The second problem is that if this is the only definition you use, it precludes all of the other definitions of miracles except for the miracles of Christ. Certainly, spontaneous remissions, modern medicine, and happy coincidences do not run counter to laws of nature.

"Setting aside the effects of sin"

Some theologians feel that in miraculous healings God isn't breaking His laws or setting aside His laws or breaking through His laws as much as He is setting aside or eliminating the effects of sin on our bodies.

Personally I have trouble with this definition. While it is true that ultimately all of the illnesses we have are the result of our living in a fallen world, I personally believe that sickness because of sin is very uncommon. In the instances in the Bible where illness was punishment for sin, there was no direct correlation between the sin that was committed and the illness that occurred.

For example, David and Bathsheba committed adultery and then David murdered Uriah, Bathsheba's husband. As a result of those sins David and Bathsheba's baby died. It was a specific and unique cause and effect, if you will. If infant mortality were the result of adultery, we would almost certainly have a declining population in the world.

King Herod accepted praise as a god and gloried in that praise and was instantly struck with worms. Yet there is no connection between vanity and political power and worm infestation. Ananias and Sapphira were both struck dead for lying to the apostles. But lying does not always lead to instant heart failure.

There is no question that some sinful behavior *leads* to illness. At last count, for example, there were twenty-six sexually transmitted diseases. Also, we have to pay the price of the physical consequences of those illnesses that we acquire from specific sinful behavior. I have never personally seen nor heard of anyone who has been miraculously healed from the type of illness that is the logical consequence of sinful behavior. I will repeat again, however, that "consequence of" is not the same as "punishment for."

In the broader sense, though, if we accept all physical illness as a consequence of living in a fallen world, which is a result of original sin, then all healing that occurs is "setting aside the effects of sin."

God "temporarily suspending natural laws"

Some theologians would say that miracles are not God breaking through or breaking His laws, but rather they are the temporary suspension of natural laws.

This is really splitting hairs. The difference between suspending laws and breaking through or breaking laws may be a fine point for debate, but when it comes to practical reality, I don't see the difference between temporarily suspending and breaking through. If you can, that is fine.

New creation

When God created the earth, He created "ex nihilo." That is a Greek term meaning "out of nothing." By just speaking, God created the universe.

In some of His miracles, Christ created things such as wine, bread, or fish "out of thin air." At other times He recreated or restored dead tissue. There is absolutely no scientific explanation for this type of "new creation," and by all accounts it is a wonderful miraculous thing.

Nothing can explain bringing truly dead tissue back to life. Nothing can restore something that has been decayed. Restoring decayed tissue to normal is a miraculous new creation.

The problem with "new creation" as a definition of a miracle is that it doesn't define all the miracles or miraculous events described in the Bible. It certainly defines the most spectacular, but all the things that were called miracles are not new creations or recreations.

Special providence

Many theologians agree that "special providence" defines special events or happenings or occurrences in our lives. Some would say the episode regarding my wife and our oldest daughter and the treatment of RhoGAM was a special providence.

When I think of this term, I think of my son Matthew. Matthew is a party animal; he is also creative. Some of the parties and events he led when he was president of the student body at Wheaton Academy are still acknowledged as the best the school has ever had. During Matt's freshman year at college, one of his best friends was having a birthday party back home, a sixty-minute drive from campus. Atypically, Matt had completed all his homework that week and was relaxing at the student center.

"Hey, Matt," said one of his buddies , "have you forgotten about the party?"

He had. Also unusual.

"Come on. We're getting ready to go," said his friend.

"I don't think I'll go," Matt said. "I don't feel like it."

This was out of character for Matt. It was his best friend's birthday party, he had planned all week to go, and he had no reason not to go, but he told them to leave without him.

Twenty minutes from campus, the boys who went were hit broadside by another car, and two of the boys were killed. Had he gone to the party, Matthew very likely would have been killed also.

To this day, Matthew can't tell you why he didn't go to that party. But it is clear to him and to us that his not getting in that car was a special providence.

But is a special providence a miracle? That's where theologians differ about the term.

Some theologians say to truly be special it has to be a direct answer to prayer or a special gift from God to you. Many of Christ's miracles were special providence and special answers to prayer and faith. Whether or not you agree with the theologians, if it is a special providence of God to you, you can and certainly should claim it as your own special miracle.

When my younger brother, Jim, was diagnosed with stomach cancer, he had the good fortune and misfortune to be in one of the first HMOs in the Chicago area. So once the diagnosis was made, he was referred to the HMO surgeon in his area. It turned out that the man had little experience in stomach cancer surgery and had a terrible bedside manner. Consequently, my brother and his wife, Carol Lou, didn't trust the man at all.

I talked to Jim and Carol Lou, and we prayed about it. I told him how to appeal to get a second opinion and to see if he could get another surgeon authorized to do his surgery. I was not a physician in that HMO nor was I affiliated with any of the hospitals he could be treated at, but I knew there was a much more experienced surgeon who was really terrific at this operation and who was on the HMO panel. One needed a special reason, however, for the HMO to refer Jim to this surgeon. We all prayed, Jim and Carol Lou appealed, and I made a few phone calls to friends to see if they could do me a favor and help in our appeal.

What it came down to was the "appellate judge," who also "happened to be" the best gastric surgeon in our city.

The HMO called him to be the arbiter and decide if the referral to this other surgeon was reasonable. Not only did this man agree with our appeal, he also volunteered to do the surgery himself.

This was an even greater answer to prayer than we dared ask for. God frequently does that, you know. He gives us more than we even dared ask for!

Signs and wonders

Christ's miracles were prophesied. The Old Testament prophets predicted that miraculous signs and wonders would be performed by the Messiah. So Christ's miracles were not only answers to prophecy, they were also special signs and wonders to prove who He was. They were proof of His divinity.

Most evangelical theologians agree that for a miracle to be a miracle it has to be a special sign of God's providence to you and God's answer to your prayers. A miracle is not just something that cannot be explained scientifically.

If you accept this definition, then something done by Satan is not a miracle. If you accept this definition, then "extraordinary intervention by supernatural powers" should be restated as "extraordinary intervention by God." Satan's acts may be signs and they may even be wondrous, but they're evil.

The miracle of salvation

In the New Testament, John 3:16, Acts 2:21, Romans 10:9, and 1 John 1:9 all describe the way to salvation: "For God so loved the world that he gave his one and only Son, that whoever believes in him shall not perish but have eternal life" (John 3:16).

Now that is a miracle!

Yet we often forget what a wonderful, miraculous, life-changing event salvation is!

I'll never forget hearing an interview with an internationally known leader of a famous alcohol and drug addiction center who stated on national television that no one can be cured of an alcohol or drug addiction before undergoing a life-changing spiritual event. I about fell out of my chair when I heard this man, an avowed atheist, say that.

Addiction counselors all over this country will tell you there is no addiction known to modern man that can be cured unless a person undergoes a life-changing spiritual experience. Now usually they are not referring to salvation in Jesus Christ! But the fact is that salvation through Jesus Christ *is* the only "authentic" spiritual experience. If even counterfeit spiritual experiences can have some healing benefits, just think how much better the "real thing" is!

I have known people addicted to cigarettes who have been instantly cured of their addiction once they were saved. Most cigarette smokers do, however, undergo agonizing physical symptoms of withdrawal. That is not to say that all cigarette smokers who are saved and want to quit smoking will be spared the physical pains or symptoms of withdrawal or even that they will instantly lose their cravings for cigarettes. Some do however. The same is true with alcohol. Some miraculously lose their craving and desire for alcohol.

Just because all don't experience this doesn't negate the miraculous life-changing event that salvation is and the curative powers salvation can have.

The same holds true for some psychological and mood disorders. Many individual sufferers have been totally cured by the salvation experience. Of course all haven't, and I don't want imply that once you are saved your psychological problems and mood disorders will be gone. But that doesn't change the fact that salvation is a miraculous event. It is miraculous that God would so love us that He would send His Son to die for us in the first place. When by grace we accept that freely given undeserved gift, it changes us physically, emotionally, socially, and every way we need to be healed.

For some this is instantaneous. For most of us it is the beginning of a long spiritual struggle. But in either case it is the ultimate life-changing event.

So my answer to the question, "Can I pray for a miracle?" is "Yes!"

And to the question, "Should I expect a miracle?" I say, "Yes!"

Miracles still happen. But that doesn't mean we will always get the miracle we want. Miracles seem to come in many forms.

The apostle Paul pleaded with God three times to be healed from a severe affliction which he termed his "thorn in my flesh." Yet God did not "take it away." God said to Paul:

"My grace is sufficient for you, for my power is made perfect in weakness." (2 Corinthians 12:9)

As a result, Paul was able to say:

Therefore I will boast all the more gladly about my weaknesses, so that Christ's power may rest on me. That is why, for Christ's sake, I delight in weaknesses, in insults, in hardships, in persecutions, in difficulties. For when I am weak, then I am strong. (12:9–10)

God may not give us the miracle we are praying for *for our own good.*

For this reason, we can't judge why one person doesn't get the miracle he or she is praying for and another does. Remember, Paul wasn't denied healing because of his lack of faith or because of unrepented sin but because of his close relationship with God and because God chose to reveal His divine power through Paul's strength and faithfulness in the midst of his weakness and affliction. And remember Job. He suffered greatly *because* he was the most righteous man in the world.

Many Christians believe that if you don't get your miracle, it is because of some unresolved sin, or lack of faith, or a combination of sin and lack of faith. My study of Scripture and my personal experience says this is not true. Satan just uses that concept to discourage us and drag us down.

Yes, we should pray for healing—for a miracle. But that is different than *demanding* healing or believing there is some magic formula for prayer we can chant so that God will grant our every prayer and wish the way we want.

Pray for healing for the woman you love. Pray for her and with her. Prayer will draw you even closer to God and to each other; both relationships will grow deeper and stronger through this tough time as you pray together.

And neither of you will ever forget the times God directly answers your prayers!

CHAPTER 17

Is It Worth It?

It hadn't been a particularly good week. In fact, it hadn't been a particularly good month. And today certainly hadn't been a particularly good day. To top it off, I had gotten home late, and Judy and I were supposed to go out to dinner with the parents of Eric Jenkinson, the young man our daughter Heather was dating seriously.

I relaxed a bit when Eric told us that his parents were hung up in traffic in Indiana. Knowing how bad the traffic usually was coming around the south side of Chicago, I thought it was a great idea when Eric suggested that we just meet his parents at the country club where we had our dinner reservations. Eric called his parents on their car phone, and they assured him they would have no difficulty finding the place.

When we got to the country club, the hostess directed us to the room where the Jenkinsons were already waiting for us.

"How'd they get here so fast?" I said. "They must have been going ninety miles an hour down the toll road!"

Then Jennifer swung the doors open and there were all of our children, my mother, my brothers and sisters, nieces and nephews, shouting, "Surprise!"

It was a few weeks before our twenty-fifth wedding anniversary, so our children had caught Judy and me totally by surprise.

What a fantastic evening! The kids put on hilarious—and insightful!—skits and parodies about our behavior and our family life. They also presented a terrific sound slide show. Altogether, it was one of the most memorable evenings of our marriage and family life. We still talk about it.

Judy and I have been blessed with the only wealth worth having: a rich family life. Our marriage has not always been easy for either of us, but nothing worth having is ever easily gained. Both of us have grown, as individuals and in our relationship. Both of us have a better understanding of who we are and why we are the people we are. And we have a wonderful mature relationship; we love each other more, we understand each other better, and we are more tolerant of each other than we ever were.

Is it all perfect? No! Do we have our ups and downs? Yes. Do I communicate as well as I should? Do I listen to my children the way I should and the way I have suggested that we all should? The answer is no, but I am trying.

You can never stop working at your marriage. Sometimes this is difficult to remember when you are in the midst of trials and pain and suffering. When your wife is ill and you're trying to keep the household running on an even keel and the kids are upset and need reassuring and you're feeling alone but are afraid to tell anyone, you can't always see the big picture. That's natural. Most of us don't at that moment.

But when that happens, sit down, catch your breath, and think about the various steps I've talked about. Then set about making a plan that will begin to meet your family's needs—including your own!

If this were your business, you would have a business plan. If it were a game, you would have a game plan. So when things get tough, sit down and map out a family plan.

How do I care for her?

How do I care for the children?

How do I care for myself?

Then pray for wisdom and help and guidance, and God will answer those prayers.

At some point, you and your wife are probably going to go through some tough times. These can come in many forms, including the particular one we have been discussing throughout this book, your wife's illness. During those times, you will need to support each other more than ever before, and often it is those very trials that truly bring you together and strengthen your relationship. Yet with the wisdom of hindsight, I offer this advice: Don't wait for the tough times to begin to understand each other's needs. Don't wait until then to learn to respect each other's desires—emotionally, physically, sexually, and every other way.

Your children will be healthier, happier, better adjusted, and better able to forge relationships if they see that lived out by their parents. Remember, what they live with they learn, what they learn they practice, what they practice they will become, what they become will have consequences for them.

If what they learn is that when times are tough you simply get a divorce, then that is what they will do also. If they see their father breaking or ignoring his marriage vows and not demonstrating love to their mother and then they hear that God our Father is love, they are going to have trouble with that concept. Not that we as parents will ever be perfect examples, but divorce and infidelity are horrible examples.

I used to hate going to weddings. I always thought they were a huge waste of time and money and that simply saying the vows in front of a minister was all that was necessary. Now that I have been the father of the bride twice, at two glorious weddings, I have changed my opinion. There is nothing as moving as a grand church wedding with great music, a short Christian homily on marriage, and the marriage vows themselves. I can barely make it through a wedding without crying now.

Marrying a fellow Christian is a mystical, spiritual, emotional, and physical bonding where two people come together, and where one and one makes more than two.

The best way to care for the woman you love is to commit to her and to pray for God's guidance and help in caring for her; those are the crucial steps that lead to true intimacy in a relationship. Then, when the tough times come or she is sick, continue to commit to her. Her knowledge of your commitment and her security in it will make a major contribution toward her healing. Not only will she be able to get better in that environment, but your relationship will grow, God will bless it, and you will be stronger because of it.

As you commit to love her without reservation, she will be able to do the same for you—not because she has to, but because she wants to. So the irony is, of course, that this is the best thing you can do for yourself as well.

The best chance you have of living a long life, the best chance you have of being successful in business, the best chance you have of having a great sex life, the best chance you have of recovering from any illness, is to have a loving wife.

Josh McDowell has said that the best thing a man can do for his children is to love their mother. I think you can expand upon this: The best thing a man can do for his community is to love his wife. The best thing a man can do for his church is to love his wife. The best thing men can do for this country is to love their wives.

God asked the ancient Israelites to love, honor, and worship Him with all their heart, mind, and soul. He asks that of us as well.

God also asks you to do the same for your wife, because your relationship with her is to be an example or a model on earth of how we are to love God and how He loves us.

Just as He blessed the ancient Israelites when they honored their vows to Him, so He will bless us as we honor our marriage vows.

My hope and prayer is that this book will in some way help you care for your wife better and help you love her more—in sickness and in health. May God bless you both richly.

> "For I know the plans I have for you," declares the Lord, "plans to prosper you and not to harm you, plans to give you hope and a future. Then you will call upon me and come and pray to me, and I will listen to you." (Jeremiah 29:11–12)

Note to the Reader

The publisher invites you to share your response to the message of this book by writing Discovery House Publishers, P. O. Box 3566, Grand Rapids, MI 49501, U.S.A. For information about other Discovery House books and music, contact us at the same address or call 1-800-653-8333.